How to Plan and Finance Your Business

How to Plan and Finance Your Business

WILLIAM R. OSGOOD

CBI

CBI PUBLISHING COMPANY, INC.
51 Sleeper Street
Boston, Mass. 02210

Production Editor: Linda Dunn McCue
Text Designer: Bywater Production Services
Compositor: Commonwealth Graphics
Dust Jacket Designer: Rosalind Schell

Library of Congress Cataloging in Publication Data

Osgood, William R

How to plan and finance your business

1. Small business—Finance. 2. Business.
I. Title.
HG4026.084 658.1′592 79-28070
ISBN 0-8436-0757-2

Printed in the United States of America

Printing *(Last Digit)*: 9 8 7 6 5 4 3 2 1

CONTENTS

ACKNOWLEDGEMENTS

This book has emerged over time, through a series of stages. Some of this material first appeared in an unpublished work by the author, *Practical Financial Management*. This work was later revised and added to with the assistance of David H. Bangs, Jr., and appeared as *The Business Planning Guide*, published first by the Federal Reserve Bank of Boston and subsequently by the Upstart Publishing Company. The material was later expanded and reorganized into its present form. Some of the material added to this major revision appeared in "Common Sense," a publication by Osgood and Bangs. Suggestions throughout this evolutionary process have been gratefully received from bankers, teachers, students, and business practioneers. Special appreciation is extended to Ann Scanlan for her continued invaluable help.

March, 1980

To the user:

This guide has been developed to assist you in constructing a logically arranged and reasonably complete business plan and financing proposal which will—

serve your need for business analysis;
serve your need for a business plan custom-designed for your business;
provide you with a set of financial forecasts based on your rational assumptions about the future and on your hard-won business experience;
set budgeting guidelines including a working capital budget and a break-even analysis for your business;
help you to determine the amount and kind of financing most appropriate to your business;
give your financing sources the most useful and persuasive information about your business to enable them to make swift, accurate, and helpful decisions.

The suggested outline is flexible and is offered as a guide which you can and should tailor to your own needs. It is based on the critical analysis and evaluation of thousands of business plans and financing proposals, and on a wide range of secondary sources such as Small Business Administration pamphlets, bank guidelines, textbooks, periodicals, and conversations with experienced proposal-writers and -readers. (See appendix D for suggested references.)

A business plan and a financing proposal are closely related. In fact, a good business plan, updated periodically, makes the most powerful financing proposal a small business can have. If you follow the guidelines (remembering to adapt them to suit your particular business situation), then you will know not only the amount of money you need to make your deal work, but also you will know and understand the kind of financing to seek and who is most likely to offer it.

This knowledge alone helps you establish credibility with the potential sources of your financing. The complete proposal, a modification of the business plan, will establish maximum credibility. By presenting a clearly thought-out, well-documented financing plan, you will show that you know what you want to do, how to do it, and how the loan will be repaid or how the investment will appreciate.

How to Use This Book

The Handbook is divided into major sections or categories, some or all of which will be useful to you, depending upon your specific needs. The first section contains a general discussion of business problems and highlights the main points of the other sections. It is intended to help identify problem areas and will help you decide which of the other sections will be most useful in problem solving. A glossary of the financial and business terminology used is included at the end of the book.

The Handbook is designed to be used both by those contemplating going into business and those already in business. The Handbook is *not* a substitute for other kinds of assistance, but rather points out the need for and strongly encourages the use of competent legal, banking, and accounting services as well as other specialized forms of assistance.

Each section of the Handbook is divided into three parts:

Major points of interest and concern, and the importance of each to the business
Procedures required to complete that section
Examples from an actual plan

If your plan requires additional information—a time/cost study, for example—include it. If, at any point in using the Handbook you need further help, *seek it out.* Various groups exist in most areas to provide free or low-cost assistance to small businesses. Ask your commercial loan officer about such organizations in your area.

When you have finished constructing your business plan, you will have a complete, coherent document which serves your needs and the needs of others who require information about your business.

Part I.
THE PLAN

1. INTRODUCTION

THE BUSINESS PLAN

Why should you go to the trouble of creating a written business plan? There are three major reasons:

1. The process of putting a business plan together, including the thought you put in before beginning to write it, forces you to take an objective, critical, unemotional look at your business project in its entirety.
2. The finished product—your business plan—is an operating tool which, properly used, will help you manage your business and work toward its success.
3. The completed business plan communicates your ideas to others and provides the basis for your financing proposal.

By taking an objective look at your business, you can identify areas of weakness and strength, pinpoint needs you might otherwise overlook, spot problems before they arise, and begin planning how you can best achieve your business goals.

As an operating tool, your business plan helps you to establish reasonable objectives and figure out how to best accomplish them. It also helps you to red-flag problems as they arise and aids you in identifying their sources, thus suggesting ways to solve them. It may even help you avoid some problems altogether.

Finally, your business plan provides the information that will be needed by others to evaluate your venture, especially if you will need to seek outside financing. A thorough business plan automatically becomes a complete financing proposal which will meet the requirements of most lenders. In order for your plan to work, it is important that you do as much of the work as possible. You must make the time available. If you are already in business, this may seem impossible. However, while you can hire people to do the work of your business, you cannot hire someone to do the planning. Others can assist you in the process, but the plan is for your business and so must be based on your ideas and assumptions. A professionally prepared business plan won't do you any good if you don't understand it thoroughly. This understanding comes from being involved with its development from the very start.

No business plan, no matter how carefully constructed and no matter how thoroughly understood, will be of any use at all unless you use it. If you are not in business but are trying to determine whether or not your business idea makes sense, or if you are getting started, the planning process outlined in this book is your most important task. It will help you avoid mistakes and will save you effort, time, and money. Going into business is rough—over half of all new businesses fail within the first two years of operation; over 90 percent fail within the first ten years. A major reason for failure is lack of planning. The best way to enhance your chances of success is to plan and follow through on your planning. Use your plan. Don't put it in the bottom drawer of your desk and forget it.

Your business plan can help you avoid going into a business venture that is doomed to failure. If your proposed venture is marginal at best, the business plan will show you why and may help you avoid paying the high tuition of business failure. It is far cheaper not to begin an ill-fated business than to learn by experience what your business plan could have taught you at a cost of several hours of concentrated work.

Plan what's going to happen—then do it.

THE FINANCING PROPOSAL

The business plan which you will develop in chapters 1 through 4 needs very little alteration to become a first-rate financing proposal. There are some areas of your plan which will be of little or no use to your banker. Personal histories, for example, can and should be replaced by a resume. The section on deviational analysis is not needed by your banker under most circumstances. The main difference between the plan and your financing proposal is one of emphasis not of design, however, and can best be understood by noticing that while the main function of a plan is to enable you to understand the complexities of the business, the function of a proposal is to show your prospective backers that you not only know what you are doing, but you will also be able to make their investment as risk-free as possible.

Most bankers deal with small-business owners who do not understand money, the differences between types of financing, and why these distinctions are important to small businesses. By showing some familiarity with the financing of a business from the banker's viewpoint, you will be on guard against two problems:

1. The banker who can't say no but who can't provide adequate financing
2. The banker who gives the wrong loan for the right reasons

Read this section carefully before customizing your plan into a proposal. The rewards may be worth the effort.

Although the greatest dollar amounts of credit for small business are found in trade credit (money owed to suppliers), the most important single financing source is your local bank. Such esoteric financing tools are factoring, discounting receivables, stocks, bonds, and other debt instruments are simply not available to most small businesses and so are not explained here. If you have need of them, your banker and accountant will help you. If you do not have both a banker and an accountant, you surely have no need of specialized financing.

The big distinction in money is:

Debt vs. Equity

When you go to the bank, you are seeking *debt money,* a loan which you repay over a period of time at a certain additional cost interest. The money you invest in your business is ordinarily *equity,* that is, money invested in a business which will not be repaid to you unless you sell a portion of your ownership. Debt financing does not lead to sharing ownership of your business with the financier; equity financing does. *Control* is another matter: your banker frequently exercises substantial control over your business through a legal document or through suggestion, but he doesn't own your business. Debt pays interest, usually for a finite period. Equity pays profits forever.

The distinction between debt and equity is of particular interest to a banker because the more debt there is in relation to equity, the higher the risk. A high debt-to-worth ratio (*worth* is roughly equivalent to equity, but includes certain kinds of specialized debt) indicates high risk. High risk costs money, if, indeed, money can be found for such a situation. Why? Because debt money is rented money, and the rent must be paid no matter what the business is doing. If you can't meet your debt payment, you go out of business.

Not only that, but a highly leveraged business—one with a higher debt/worth ratio than normal for that kind of business—must earn more money. Sometimes a small-business owner, having read books on getting rich using other people's money, will find so much debt money that he can never get ahead no matter how hard he works; without capital, permanent, nonrepayable money invested in the business, he'll spin his wheels forever, a problem called *overtrading.* The trade ratios of sales/worth are guidelines to follow here (Barometer, Robert Morris, Dun & Bradstreet).

From a banker's viewpoint, the higher the debt, the riskier the deal. The longer the term of the debt, the riskier the deal. Short-term loans are less hazardous than long-term (with some exceptions) because, if the loan goes sour, it does so in a hurry and can be easily detected, while a long-term decline can be almost imperceptible. The underlying issue is that performance in the near future can be predicted with much greater certainty than in longer time frames. Risk represents the odds against an expected happening occurring in the future.

The key here is to fit the financing to the need. When you project your cash flow, you will do two things which will help decide what kind of financing you need: the sum of the negative cash flow will indicate the amount of money you need in some combination of debt and equity, while the projected cash receipts show how you will generate money to repay any debt you incur. If you don't arrange for enough financing, from whatever sources, your deal will be dead. If you borrow more than you can service, your deal will also be dead. For any kind of bank financing, Friday-night financing never works. Always make sure your banker knows what your needs will be well in advance. Then you won't get caught in a cash squeeze which could be prevented by careful nurturing of your business and your banker. Borrowing under panic conditions is outrageously dangerous. Don't do it. This, of course, carries right along with our advice for planning throughout the guide.

Earlier in this section, we mentioned the problems of the banker who can't say no but who won't provide the right amount of money. If you have thought through your business plan, you know how much you need: make sure to get it; less will only make your life difficult if not impossible. If your banker can give good reason for you to borrow less, pay attention but think it over. Do not settle for enough money to get you in trouble but not enough to see you through.

Also, by knowing what you are borrowing money for, and knowing how the loan will earn its repayment, you will avoid getting caught in the wrong loan. Tell your banker what you need the money for and what you think the loan should look like; listen to his reasoning if he disagrees—but make sure, absolutely sure, that you will not find yourself committed to repaying a loan faster than your cash flow can handle, nor paying for a dead horse years after the purchase has been used up. There is a middle course, a responsible one which will make the business safter, less risky, more profitable, and more fun.

Take that middle way: plan, know what the loan is for, how you will pay it back, and be realistic about the risk. This way, you won't have any surprises and you will be in control of the situation rather than having the situation control you.

A final reminder: Planning is the key to business success.

The plan format

The information and ideas collected during the planning process take a particular form when organized into the business plan. This material should be organized in a rational order so that it leads the reader from point to point to a logical conclusion. The sequence is important because each idea and each section builds on the one before. The suggested outline on page 000 is the result of reviewing and evaluating literally thousands of plans; it is designed to satisfy the requirements of most lenders, especially commercial bankers and the Small Business Administration.

Certain material in the business plan is designed to set the stage. This material, called the front matter, includes the cover sheet, the statement of purpose, and the table of contents. The statement of purpose is especially important as an introduction to the plan; it informs the reader what to expect. Explanation and samples of the front matter is included in Appendix A.

The planning process does not guarantee your way to success, but it will substantially reduce your chances of failure. The business plan is hard work and requires much thought and attention, but, the dividends will far outweigh the costs.

Suggested outline for the business plan

- * Cover sheet: Name of business, names of principals, address and phone number of business
- * Statement of purpose
- * Table of contents

I. The Business
  - A. Description
  - B. Market
  - C. Competition
  - D. Location
  - E. Management
  - F. Personnel
  - G. Application and expected effect of loan (if needed)
  - H. Summary

II. Financial Data
  - A. Sources and applications of funding
  - B. Capital equipment list
  - C. Balance sheet
  - D. Break-even analysis
  - E. Income projections (pro forma income statements)
    1. Three-year summary
    2. Detail by month, first year
    3. Detail by quarter, second and third years
    4. Notes of explanation
  - F. Pro forma cash flow analysis
    1. Detail by month, first year
    2. Detail by quarter, second and third years
    3. Notes of explanation
  - G. Deviation analysis
  - H. Historical financial reports for existing business
    1. Balance sheets for past three years
    2. Income statements for past three years
    3. Tax Returns

III. Supporting Documents: Personal resumes, job descriptions, personal financial statements, credit reports, letters of reference, letters of intent, copies of leases, contracts, legal documents, and anything else of relevance to the plan.

*For discussion and samples of the cover sheet, statement of purpose, and table of contents, see Appendix A.

1. THE BUSINESS

To describe your business is the most important and most difficult part of your business plan. The objective of this section is to make a clear statement of—

1. What the business is or will be;
2. What market you intend to service, the size of the market, and your expected share;
3. Why you can service that market better than your competition;
4. Why you have chosen your particular location;
5. What management and other personnel are available and required for the operation;

   If you are preparing a financing proposal, include—

6. Why debt money or someone's equity investment will make your business more profitable.

The six considerations are the written *policy* of your business. They are rules you should not deviate from without compelling reasons. *Policy* gives direction and stability to your business. As such, it requires a great deal of thought and planning. This section can help you establish *policy.* You may disagree with the suggestions and examples given; the suggestions offered are only ideas you might find helpful. Your business will reflect your personality and abilities, not someone else's. In describing your business idea, aim at clarity and simplicity. A rule of thumb: if you can't describe your idea clearly and simply, you haven't thought it through.

Remember that technical support for your business idea will be found primarily in the *financial data* section and the *supporting documents.* For now, reference the supporting data as needed. Too much detail here gets in the way of explaining your idea.

A. DESCRIPTION

The objective of this section is to show what your business is, how you are going to run it, and why you think your business will be successful (see Figure 1-1).

Figure 1-1. Sample description of business

Finestkind Seafoods, Inc., is a fish market specializing in selling extremely fresh (no more than one day from the boat) seafood to both retail and wholesale customers. At present, 60 percent of sales are to retail customers. Finestkind Seafoods plans to concentrate more heavily on the wholesale trade (restaurants and grocery chains) in the future. Our experience has shown that even though the markup is lower for wholesale trade, profits are higher due to lower personnel costs and faster turnover of inventory.

Finestkind Seafoods, Inc., began business in September, 19-, and is open seven days a week from 10:00 a.m. to 8:30 p.m. for retail business and from 6:00 a.m. to 8:30 p.m. for wholesale. The retail demand is seasonal and fluctuates according to weather (our store is located on a tourist route). The wholesale demand is constant and increasing. We feel that the latter can be improved by more direct selling. Our customers agree (see letters from Nightlife Clambake and Grandiose Suprettes in the supporting documents). The quality of our seafood is exceptional, and, since Mr. Swan is a former fisherman with many personal friends in the fishing industry, we do not anticipate difficulty maintaining good relations with our suppliers. We have made a policy of paying premium prices in cash at dockside for the best, freshest fish.

Deciding what your business is now—and what it will be in three years—is the most important decision you will have to make. A small, ongoing business may be involved in more than one activity. If so, your determination and description of the central activity (or central activities) are crucial. Your entire planning effort is based on your perception of what business you are in. If you make a serious error at this point, your chances of success will be sharply diminished. So be sure to take the time to think this decision through.

The description includes—

1. the type of business: primarily merchandising, manufacturing, or service;
2. the status of business: a start-up; an expansion of a going concern; a take-over of an existing business;
3. the business form: sole proprietorship, partnership, corporation—(ask your attorney's advice);
4. the reason(s) your business will be profitable;
5. the opening date, future or past;
6. the hours of the day and days of the week you will be (you are) in operation. Note: If yours is a seasonal business, or if the hours will be adjusted seasonally, make sure that the seasonality is reflected in your replies to 5 & 6.

Item 1 is your description of the central activity of your business; it involves more detail than a simple statement like, "Finestkind Seafoods, Inc., is a merchandising operation concentrating on seafoods," (see Figure 1-1). Knowing exactly what your business does and how it operates enables you to plan for profits effectively. Before you begin to consider profit-making, you must be able to identify clearly the aims and goals of your business. Once you are sure of these, you can figure out how to make profits. As the business progresses, the question of how to make profits must continually be asked and answered. The answers will help you identify what is special about your business and why it won't be one of the 50 percent or more that fail during their first two years.

You will not complete item 4 until you finish the income projections section in Chapter 2. The reasons should emerge as your business plan progresses.

Items 5 & 6 are particularly important for merchandising and service businesses. These are critical marketing concerns which will be further considered in the next section.

Since start-ups and take-overs face different kinds of problems, each is treated separately on the following pages. The checklists provided are in addition to Items 1 through 6.

For a new business

Your description of the business should contain responses to the following (as well as the six items previously listed):

7. Why will you be successful in this business?
8. What is your experience in this business?
9. Have you spoken with other people in this kind of business? What was their response?
10. What will be special about your business?

Many new businesses fail to take advantage of the insights and experience of possible competitors. They are your best single source of information and will often give you much valuable advice for nothing more than a chance to show their expertise. Talking with them and observing their business practices will also help you define what the special advantages of your own business will be.

11. Have you spoken with prospective trade suppliers to find out what managerial and/or technical help they will provide?
12. Have you asked about trade credit?

Trade credit is a source of funds. Payment terms such as "net due in thirty days" (N/30) allow you to use the supplier's money for the thirty days—it's like an interest-free loan for that period. However, doing this means that you forego the cash discount frequently available if the bill is paid within ten days. Taking the discount can represent a substantial savings on the cost of the supplier's product: if the terms are 2/10, N/30, you save 2 percent of net by paying within ten days. The cash discount represents an annualized interest rate of 72 percent. If you can borrow funds elsewhere for less interest, you should take advantage of the savings. Such credit is often not available until a business has been in operation for a length of time sufficient to establish a reputation for paying on time. Many suppliers also offer free services as an inducement to buy their product. For instance, store-fixture manufacturers give free layout advice; utility companies give hints on how the effective use of light can create more sales.

13. If you will be doing any contract work, what are the terms? Reference any firm contract or letter of intent, and include it as a supporting document.

This is especially important for anyone contemplating contract work: find out how and when you will be paid. Get a feel from other contractors about their experiences. A slow-paying customer can put you out of business if you aren't prepared. If slow payment is a fact of life for your business,

14. How will you offset the slow payment by the customer?

For a take-over

Your description of business should contain a brief history of the business you plan to take over and include responses to the following questions in addition to the first six items:

15. When and by whom was the business founded?
16. Why is the owner selling it?
17. How did you arrive at a purchase price for the business?

Businesses which are strong and growing are rarely offered for sale, and most sellers will give—though not necessarily deliberately—misleading reasons for selling their business. Protect yourself. Ask your banker to check out the business. This is a normal activity for him, and he has the means available to find out information you may not be able to get. If your lawyer or accountant is experienced, ask him. Pricing a business requires professional expertise and ethics. Paying for a professional appraisal may turn out to be an excellent investment as it not only establishes a fair price for the business but also provides justification for the price if outside financing is needed. Include a copy of the appraisal as a supporting document. The price should reflect the assets of the business, the rate of expected income on your investment, and perhaps a goodwill factor (sometimes a business has patents which can be capitalized, an excellent reputation for service, or an advantageous lease).

Since you will be repaying the purchase price out of profit, make sure that you are getting what you are paying for.

18. What is the trend of sales?
19. If the business is going downhill, why? How can you turn it around?
20. How will your management make the business more profitable?

Items 18 & 19 should be supported by income statements and tax returns. Remember, if a business is sliding downhill, there may be reasons which aren't immediately obvious. Check out the owner's reasons. Ask his bankers. It is difficult to restore a tarnished reputation, and it can't be done overnight.

Some additional thoughts to keep in mind as you check out the business: Have you evaluated and aged the inventory? checked with trade creditors? aged the receivables? what is the condition and age of operating machinery? does the business owe money—and, if it does, will you inherit the liabilities?

Determine exactly what you are buying. You are planning to put your money on the line. Don't be afraid to ask for advice before you commit yourself to any deal. A good attorney is essential to help determine what you are buying and to make sure that the terms of the sale are in your favor.

Note that the description in Figure 1-1 covers most of the points on these checklists. The checklists provide a guideline, not a straitjacket.

It should be apparent that Finestkind has a well-defined strategy. The owners will be selling premium quality seafood to two target markets: wholesale (restaurants, markets, institutions) and retail (mainly tourists at the 123 Fish Lane store). In the future, they will concentrate more heavily on the wholesale market since they feel their chances of penetrating that market are better than their chances of increasing their retail trade. Shifting a target market has problems, but doing so deliberately and thoughtfully makes such a shift more manageable. This shift would be most hazardous if done without a clear idea of where the business is, where it makes the most profit, and where it is heading.

Finestkind should be prepared to explain to a loan officer what exceptional quality is and how they expect to be competitive if they continue to pay premium prices for their seafood. These are the areas in which Finestkind is special (distinguished from their competitors), but it may prove to be economically self-defeating.

B. MARKET

Figure 1-2. Sample statement for market section

Finestkind Seafoods, Inc., will continue to provide premium quality seafoods to both wholesale (restaurants and markets) and retail customers, emphasizing the former. Our goal is to provide the freshest seafood at competitive prices to customers within twenty-five miles of Port Lobster. This market has a total population of over 100,000 people and a potential of 300 wholesale customers (see excerpt from the Census Report in the supporting documents). Customers will be attracted by: (1) direct approach to restaurants and markets; (2) a local radio and newspaper advertising campaign; (3) word-of-mouth advertising from our current customer base, and (4) our location on a heavily traveled tourist route.

The objective of this section is to make a clear statement of your market and your marketing strategy, (see Figure 1-2).

The basic marketing considerations are:

1. Who is your market?
2. What is the present size of the market?
   What percent of the market will you have?
   What is the market's growth potential?
   As the market grows, does your share increase or decrease?
3. How will you satisfy your market?
4. How will you price your service, product, or merchandise to make a fair profit and, at the same time, be competitive?

Many businessmen, the more successful ones, consider marketing skills to be of prime importance. Once you clearly identify the market you wish to service, you can focus on these items in a coherent way. Your first problem, then, is to:

Define your market

This market is the *target* for all of your efforts. Define the target market logically by considering: Who needs your service? Who needs your product? Who buys the kind of merchandise you stock? Your target market may be defined by geographic location, socioeconomic or ethnic factors, age, sex, or any of a thousand other conditions. Whatever it is, make sure you identify it. One way to do this is simply to list all of the important characteristics and then, by using census data or other information, find out to what extent these characteristics are present in different areas. It may prove necessary to change your service, product, or merchandise mix to meet the needs of the market you have targeted (Item 3) or make rational price adjustments (Item 4). However, you first must know exactly who your market is.

Measuring your target market

Your target market, the market you have selected to serve, must be measured. Having too few customers puts you out of business. Although your business will receive cash from four sources—(1) sales, (2) loan proceeds, (3) sale of fixed assets, and (4) proceeds of new investment—it will ultimately rely on sales as the main source. If there are no sales, there is no business. You can obtain information about the size of your market from your chamber of commerce, trade publications, marketing consultants, and other business people, schools, and colleges. An excellent source of information is the federal census report which includes your area; you will find one in the nearest library. Get help in assessing the market from such sources; do not try to guess by watching passing traffic and hoping for the best. Good marketing strategy must be planned, and the plan must be based on good information.

Satisfying your market

When you have a feeling for your market, the following questions can be raised. The answers help you formulate one aspect of your marketing strategy.

5. How will you attract and keep this market?
6. How can you expand your market?

Satisfying your market should be part of your basic company policy. Finestkind Seafoods has product freshness as a policy, not a temporary strategy (see Figure 1-1). Items 5 and 6 focus on such ideas as how and where to advertise, the suitability of your location, and the attractiveness and comfort of your store for the clientele you hope to acquire.

Pricing your market

The second aspect of your marketing strategy concerns price:

7. What price do you anticipate getting for your product?
8. Is the price competitive?
9. Why will someone pay your price?
10. How did you arrive at the price? Is it profitable?
11. What special advantages do you offer that may justify higher prices? (You don't necessarily have to engage in direct price competition.)

In order to make a profit, a business must make more on sales than it spends, both directly, as in cost of goods sold, and indirectly, as in overhead and selling costs. Many businesses flounder because they lose sight of this simple truth.

The key to Finestkind's pricing strategy (Figure 1-7) is that it is pegged to competitive prices. For most small businesses, this is the safest pricing strategy: What do the competitors charge? Can you make a profit at that price? Can you justify a different price (by lower costs, for example, or higher quality or more service)? Keep in mind that pricing reflects a total package of product and service and expenses. There is no point in pricing yourself out of the market, nor is there anything to be gained from a price which puts your business in the red.

Your marketing strategy also must include plans for credit.

12. Will you offer credit to your customers?

If you give credit to your customers, you are, in effect, making a loan to them. Determine if you can afford to do this, if you have to extend credit, if you can evaluate credit risk, if you can collect, and if you can afford to write off bad debts. Customer credit can represent an unexpected cash drain on the business. If you must offer credit, make sure that you plan how to absorb its effects. Offering credit to your customers costs you money, especially if you have to borrow funds to cover these accounts. Credit may strangle your business by tying up funds you could possibly use for other purposes.

Note that Finestkind has included in its statement both policy and strategies consistent with that policy (see Figure 1-2). Finestkind's marketing strategy is limited to a specific area, the area the owners feel they can service without incurring prohibitive travel and spoilage costs. Their advertising will be on local radio stations (there are four 1,000 KW stations which cover the area effectively without being too expensive) and in local papers. Advertising costs money, and they plan to spend their advertising budget wisely.

C. COMPETITION

If you have decided on your target market and that it is large enough to be profitable and contains reasonable expansion possibilities, the next step is to check out your competition, both direct (similar operations) and indirect. Consider these questions:

1. Who are your five nearest competitors?

2. How will your operation be better than theirs?
3. How is their business: steady? increasing? decreasing? Why?
4. How are their operations similar and dissimilar to yours?
5. What are their strengths and/or weaknesses?
6. What have you learned from watching their operations?

The objective of this section is to enable you to make a clear judgment and statement of how you will make your business more profitable by picking up the good competitive practices and by avoiding the errors of your competitors (see Figure 1-3). A common error is opening a business in a market that is already more than adequately serviced. Carefully evaluating the competition will sometimes lead you to alter your basic business strategy or change existing operations to compete more effectively.

The number of competitors (five) in Item 1 is arbitrary. Use your own judgment. Perhaps you have no direct competitors (Finestkind has only three), only indirect. But make sure you keep abreast of the competition on a regular basis—at least quarterly, preferably more often. Evaluating your competition should be an ongoing practice since markets shift and success attracts competition.

Figure 1-3. Sample statement for competition section

There are three seafood operations directly competing with Finestkind Seafoods.

1. Fred's Fish—scattered operation with one truck making the rounds and a small counter leased from a supermarket in Pig Gut Village. We have cut into their sales by making promised deliveries on time and at the agreed price. As a result, their operation has become marginal.
2. Kingfisher—clean, three-man operation specializing in cheaper fish. Have trouble with their suppliers because they aren't willing to pay top dockside prices. Otherwise, sell directly to housewives from a fleet of three trucks, have some wholesale trade which they hope to expand. Their sales are apparently expanding because they have been serving the same routes for five years and have an excellent reputation. Located in Rye.
3. Jonah's Seafoods—good relations with suppliers, has most of the supermarket trade, no retail. Currently rebuilding due to disastrous fire but will be our most serious competition when his new store opens. Twenty-five years of experience in the Pig Gut/Port Lobster area, good location on scenic bridge over Pig Gut Inlet two miles south of Finestkind on tourist route; plans to open retail store and may be willing to give up part of wholesale since he is getting on in years.

The indirect competition is from the major processors in Portland (forty-five miles east) and Boston (sixty miles south). Since we fall between their primary market areas, we can purchase from both on consignment basis.

By evaluating the competition, Finestkind can find ways to serve its chosen market better and to plan for the future. The owners plan to learn from the other persons' mistakes and to go after the market segment which is currently being inadequately served (in this case, the wholesale trade). A good practice to follow is to identify an unserved or undersatisfied target market, specifically identify the needs of that target market, and go after it. An advantage for a small business is its ability to operate profitably in a market too small for big businesses to consider. Checking out the competition is a valuable extension of your marketing efforts.

D. LOCATION

Proper site location can help your business make money. The objective of this section is to make a clean statement of how your location suits your business (see Figure 1-4).

Figure 1-4. Sample statement for location section

Finestkind is currently leasing a one-story, wooden frame building with cement floor (2,000 square feet) at 123 Fish Lane, Port Lobster, New Hampshire, for $175 per month with an option to buy at $22,000 (in writing). The area is zoned for commercial use. Fish Lane is part of U.S. Route 1, a heavily traveled tourist route with most businesses nearby catering to the tourist trade. Finestkind has performed major leasehold improvements including rough-sawn, pine board walls, and installation of a walk-in freezer. The building is divided into: (1) sales/counter area (1,200 square feet); (2) cutting area (100 square feet); and (3) other (space for toilet, potential storage and/or sales area totaling 700 square feet). See diagram included in supporting documents.

If you are going into business, first try to locate the ideal site, then determine how close you can come to it, remembering that rent is the combination of space and advertising.

Information about specific areas is available from chambers of commerce, trade sources such as magazines and associations, planning commissions, bankers, and lawyers. Industrial development commissions may also have information about tax breaks and financing incentives for businesses which will employ substantial numbers of people in towns under their commission. Traffic studies which can answer questions about location may be available for the area you are interested in. Other sources of this information are the state or local highway agencies, the local library, chambers of commerce, and large stores. Your local banker may well be your most useful reference. Some locations seem to be jinxed, and most likely he will know why and will tell you. Do not go into business in a given spot simply because the price is low. Rent and purchase prices are usually fixed by market forces, and a low price can reflect low desirability.

Once you get started, or if you are already located, keep a constant eye on changes in your location—new roads get built, populations shift from one class to another, people move, zoning ordinances change, and your business needs may alter, too. Prepare to anticipate these changes. For example, compare census reports over a period of time to see long-range shifts. Try to find other current data that will help you be aware of these changes.

Different businesses have different location needs. If the enterprise is manufacturing or wholesale, low rent and easy access to transportation routes are very important. For most retail operations, exposure and accessibility are most important.

In this section of your business plan, you should answer the following:

1. What is your business address?
2. What are the physical features of your building?
3. Is your building leased or owned? State the terms.
4. If renovations are needed, what are they? What is the expected cost? Get quotes in writing from more than one contractor; include quotes as supporting documents.
5. What is the neighborhood like? Does the zoning permit your kind of business?
6. What kind of businesses are in the area?
7. Have you considered other areas? Why is this site desirable for your business?
8. Why is this the right building and location for your business?
9. How does this location affect your operating costs?

The key to correct site selection is to keep in mind that a bad site can put you out of business, while a good site can increase your profits.

This section requires only a brief statement whenever you update your business plan. It may also serve as a reminder of things to look out for once a location has been chosen. You may not make suggested alterations for reasons which you forget between periods of updating your plan, so it may be wise to make a note of them as they are brought up.

E. MANAGEMENT

According to various studies of factors causing small-business failures, roughly 98 percent of businesses fail because of managerial weakness; less than 2 percent of the failures are due to factors beyond control of the persons involved. The objective of this section is to make a statement of both strengths and weaknesses of management. Keep this section short, direct, and honest (see Figure 1-5).

Your business plan must take this into account. If you are preparing a financing proposal, you should make sure that your prospective financing source is aware of what steps you have taken or are taking to correct any weaknesses in your managerial staff (yourself and any other managerial persons involved). Highlighting these strengths and weaknesses enables you to use your business plan to its fullest extent.

Figure 1-5. Sample statement for management section

Mr. Gosling was born in Port Lobster and has lived there all his life. After graduating from Port Lobster schools and serving in the United States Navy for three years, he became a self-employed carpenter, taking night courses in small-business management and sales at Pig Gut State, with the ultimate aim of owning and managing a retail store. He also serves as a member of the zoning board for Port Lobster. He and his wife (a medical secretary) live in Port Lobster with their two children.

Mr. Swan was born in Zilch, Wisconsin, in 19--, attended schools in Utah, Alaska, and Florida, and served four years in the Marines (rank upon separation, E-3). He test-drove motorcycles for a year, then served as parts manager for Wheely Cycles, Inc., before joining the Fatback

Fishfood Division of Grandiose Foodstuff, Inc., as a packer in March 1973, in the East Machias, Maine, plant. In June 1975, he resigned as line foreman of the Frozen Food Filleting Department to join Mr. Gosling in the Finestkind operation. He is unmarried and lives in Pig Gut.

Both men are healthy and energetic; they believe their abilities complement each other and will permit them to make Finestkind a success. In particular, Mr. Swan knows all of the fishermen while Mr. Gosling is well-known by the entire community. Since Mr. Swan has had experience in cost control and line management, he will be responsible for the store and inventory control. Mr. Gosling will be primarily responsible for the development of the wholesale business and, with Mr. Swan, will set policy. Personnel decisions will be made jointly.

Salaries will be $215/month for the first year to enable the business to pay off startup costs. Mr. Gosling's wife earns enough to support his family; Mr. Swan's personal expenditures are very low since he shares a house with five other unmarried men. In the second year, they will earn $600/month; in the third year, $660/month, with any profit returned to the business.

In order to augment their skills, Mr. Gosling and Mr. Swan have enlisted the help of Scrooge Farley, CPA, and Mason Petrocelli, Esq. Other potential resources have been located and spoken with, including the Port Lobster Business Information Center (Andrew O'Bangfo), Pig Gut State's Venture Incubator Division (Dr. Good), the Smaller Business Association of New England, and the Fish Retailers Organized for Growth (FROG). Marshall Sailor, a retired Port Lobster banker, has agreed to serve on the Finestkind Board and will provide ongoing management review. Other members of the Board are Farley, Petrocelli, Gosling, and Swan.

The failure-factor breakdown provides a guide:

Managerial incompetence	45%
Inexperience in the line	9%
Inexperience in management	18%
Unbalanced expertise	20%
Neglect of business	3%
Fraud	2%
Disaster	1%
Total	98%

There is no known cure for incompetence, but there are very direct cures for inexperience or unbalanced expertise: (1) get the necessary experience yourself, or (2) find a partner or employee who has the requisite experience. Almost always, managerial failures because of neglect, fraud, or disaster could have been presented by foresight. Insurance is only one example of foresight.

The management section covers five areas:

1. Personal history of principals
2. Related work experience
3. Duties and Responsibilities
4. Salaries
5. Resources available to the business

Properly treated, these five areas will help make a proposal more convincing and a business plan far more useful than could otherwise be the case. The aim is to spot areas of potential weakness before these problems put you out of business.

Personal history of principals

This segment should include responses to the following questions:

1. What is your business background?
2. What management experience have you had?
3. What education have you had (including both formal and informal learning experiences) which have bearing on your managerial abilities?
4. What is your personal background? State your age, where you live and have lived, your special abilities and interests, your reasons for going into business.

The personal data needn't be a confession, but it should reflect your motivation. Without strong motivation, your chances of success are slight. It pays to be ruthlessly honest with yourself even if you don't put all the results on paper.

5. Are you physically up to the job? Stamina counts.
6. Why are you going to be successful at this venture?

Keep in mind that your family will be affected by your decision to go into business for yourself and try to assess the potential fallout; while they may be supportive now, will they continue to be?

7. A personal financial statement must be included as a supporting document in your business plan if it is a proposal for financing.

Bankers and other lending sources want to see as much collateral as possible to secure their loan. Be forewarned: Under most circumstances, the personal creditworthiness of the principals will be a major concern of the banker. Also, you will undoubtedly be expected to sign personally for the loan. This means that your personal assets may be taken if the business fails, even if the business is a corporation.

Related work experience

This segment is a detailed response to the experience factors mentioned earlier. It includes, but is not limited to, responses to the following:

1. What is your direct operational experience in this type of business?
2. What is your managerial experience in this type of business?
3. What is your managerial experience acquired elsewhere—whether in totally different kinds of businesses, or as an offshoot of club or team membership, civic activities, church work, or some other.

Some managerial skills are transferable, others are not. Unbalanced managerial experience can cause serious problems. For example, the talents required of a financial specialist are quite different from those of a used-car salesman. A combination of both sets of talents in one individual is rare.

Duties and responsibilities

Once you have written down the experience and skills of the proposed management and have a feel for the weaknesses, this segment becomes much simpler. The rule to follow is *always build on strengths and seek to alleviate weaknesses.* This is a variant on "You can't make a silk purse of a sow's ear." Attempting to make a salesman out of a retiring clerk is folly. Attempting to make a sales manager out of your star salesman may also be folly. Use skills to advantage.

The scarcest asset you will have is time. To make the most of it, make sure that you budget your time carefully by spelling out, in advance, who does what; who reports to whom; and where the final decisions are made. Include—

1. time for planning and reviewing plans;
2. major operating duties (purchasing, sales, personnel, promotion, production, and so forth as appropriate for your business);
3. *planning.*

The purpose of your plan is to make business run more smoothly. If you find you spend a lot of [illegible]terday's problems, stop; get out of the shop; sit down and [illegible]rpetually run in circles.

[illegible]onsibilities is critical. If the chain of command is unclear to [illegible]e worst kinds of personnel problems. This is a major re[illegible] must not be evaded with the statement, "We can work it [illegible]e problems are."

Salaries

[illegible]anagement will be paid is sufficient. Cut the fat from [illegible]ent for contingencies, and then stick to it. Many deals [illegible] feel the principals are getting paid more than they [illegible]en the rock-bottom figure, unrealistic to begin with, is [illegible]wing the business budget out of kilter. Be realistic, but [illegible]in the future—after the business becomes successful.

Resources available to the business

A[illegible], need—

1. An accountant
2. A lawyer
3. An insurance broker

If you don't have these, get them *immediately.*

Other sources of assistance include:

4. Business-information centers
5. Chambers of commerce, regional planning commissions and councils
6. Business, trade, and civic organizations, which often have a pool of talent available to their members
7. Small Business Administration technical assistance, ACE, and SCORE programs
8. Consultants
9. Colleges, universities, and schools
10. Federal, state, and local agencies
11. Your board of directors (if appropriate)

Don't forget your banker. He can be the most helpful because of his job. If you are borrowing money from him or banking at his bank, he has a vested interest in the success of your business.

You won't necessarily have to use all of these resources (except the lawyer, accountant and insurance broker), but it is a good idea to know what help will be available if you need it, and to know where it is well ahead of time.

Listing these resources will make you aware of the availability of management skills in your business and available to you outside your business. Make yourself known to them; you can plug many gaps in your experience and increase your chances of success. Using them will cost you no more than time and a phone call.

By keeping in mind the necessity of managing your business rather than letting the business manage you, and by constantly reviewing and re-evaluating the results of this analysis in the future, you will drastically shorten the odds against you.

F. PERSONNEL

Businesses stand or fall on the strength of their personnel. The objective of this section is to determine and give a clear statement of your present and future hiring needs (see Figure 1-6). Good employees can make a marginal deal go; poor employees can destroy the best business. Studies have consistently shown that out of 100 customers who stop patronizing the average store, over 70 do so because they didn't get prompt, courteous attention. Here are some questions to think about in determining your hiring needs:

1. What are your personnel needs now? In the near future? In five years?
2. What skills must they have?
3. Are the people you need available?
4. Will you employ them full- or part-time?
5. What are their salaries or hourly wages?
6. What are their fringe benefits?

7. Will you require overtime?
8. Will you have to train people? If so, at what cost to the business (both time of more experienced workers and money)?

Be careful. Training personnel can be a hidden cost that you haven't counted on.

One excellent personnel control is the job description. Hire people only when it will result in added profitability to your business, and think before hiring whether the job is really necessary. If it is, then careful selection of a person to fill the job will more than repay the time and effort involved in hiring the best person for that job. There are standard application forms you may find useful in the selection process. You should also check with the SBA for their booklets on personnel management as well as your local Department of Employment Security and perhaps buy a copy of *Personnel for the Small Business* from the *Small Business Reporter,* Department 3120, Bank of America, P.O. Box 370005, San Francisco, California 94137 (this will cost $1.00).

Figure 1-6. Sample statement for personnel section

Finestkind will hire one part-time salesperson within six months whose duties will be selling seafoods over the counter to the retail customers. He or she will be paid the minimum wage ($2.30/hour) for weekend work; no fringe benefits or overtime are anticipated. We will also employ, on an as-needed basis, one cutter at $3.75/hour to help prepare seafood for the wholesale trade.

G. APPLICATION AND EXPECTED EFFECT OF LOAN OR INVESTMENT

This section is important, whether you are seeking a loan or planning to finance your deal yourself. The objective of this section is to determine how much money you will need and for what purposes it will be used (see Figure 1-7). Do not rely on guesses when exact prices or firm estimates are available. If you must make an estimate, specify how you arrived at your figures. It may be helpful to make a three-column list:

Bare Bones	*Reasonable*	*Optimal*
What you can just scrape by with—secondhand, makeshift—the bare minimum.	What you will most likely get—some new, some used, some fancy, and some plain.	What you'd like if money were no problem and you weren't worried about making a profit.
Examples	*Examples*	*Examples*
Bicycle with large basket (Schwinn '52 @ $12.50)	Pick-up truck with insulated camper adapted to icing fish (used Ford @ $1,885)	Custom-made El Dorado with mobile refrigeration unit (Cadillac custom @ $18,500)
Used desk @ $7	Renovated desk @ $25	Custom teak desk @ $750

Fill out the bare bones and optimal columns first, then make your reasonable choice. It may be important to you to have a luxury item or two, but weigh the cost. This tabular worksheet is particularly useful for a start-up business and can be used whenever a purchase of additional equipment is contemplated.

Make sure that this section contains responses to the following:

1. How is the loan or investment to be spent? This can be fairly general (working capital and new equipment, inventory, supplies).
2. What is the item or items to be bought?
3. Who is the supplier?
4. What is the price?
5. What is the specific model name and/or number of your purchase(s)?
6. How much did you (will you) pay in sales tax, installation charges, and/or freight fees?

Your banker may be interested in using the item that you are buying as collateral for the loan. If you provide a list, your loan can be processed faster.

You should consider the possible advantages of leasing some of the capital equipment you need and assess the advantages of renting rather than owning your business building. If you have the money to buy, owning may be less expensive than leasing; it may not be—ask your accountant. If you are short of cash, a lease arrangement may enable you to ease your cash problems by lowering your investment in fixed assets (perhaps a sale/lease back deal). Leases also have greater flexibility: as your business grows, you can often make changes more readily. It is also possible to save money on taxes by deducting lease payments as business expenses. The technique of break-even analysis is of great help in making a decision of this kind (see chapter 4).

Most importantly, ask yourself:

7. How will the loan make the business more profitable?

Interest is an expense which reduces profits. If you propose borrowing money or investing your own, you must know how the money is going to work for you. Make sure the money you use earns more than it costs.

Figure 1-7. Sample statement for application and expected effect of loan

The $36,000 will be used as follows:

Purchase of 123 Fish Lane property	$22,000
Equipment	
Used Ford pick-up with insulated body	1,885
Dayton compressor (used, serial #45-cah-990)	115
Sharp Slicer (used, Speedy model)	200
Renovations (see contractor's letter in supporting documents)	4,000
Working capital	4,000
Inventory	500
Reserve (not disbursed)	3,300
Total	$36,000

Finestkind Seafoods, Inc., can purchase the 125 Fish Lane property at a substantial savings under terms of the lease/purchase agreement signed July, 19--. An independent appraiser has calculated the value of the property, including leasehold improvements by Finestkind, at $30,000. The monthly payment for a twelve-year mortgage will be $250/month, a net increase of $75/month over the current year. See financial data for the effect on the business.

The truck will be used to deliver merchandise to our wholesale customers, retard spoilage, and maintain the quality of our merchandise.

The compressor will replace the compressor now used for our refrigeration unit and should lower electric costs.

The slicer will eliminate four man-hours of work daily. The time released will be used for soliciting more business and processing a greater volume of whole fish. With the slicer, relatively untrained help can fillet flounder with minimal waste.

The renovations are: a deep well (water) required by the state, a toilet and wash sink separate from the work area, and replacement of the current, obsolete heating system, which will reduce fuel expenses.

The working capital will enable Finestkind to meet current expenses, offset negative (seasonal) cash flow as shown in the Working Capital Analysis in Financial Data, and insure the continued growth of the business.

The inventory is to take advantage of bulk rates on certain fresh-frozen packaged goods such as baitfish and South African lobster tails.

The reserve will be held by the bank as a line of credit to be used to take advantage of special opportunities or to meet emergencies.

The sample shown in Figure 1-7 is modest; for a more complicated deal, much more detail would be needed. Be guided by your judgment in this section. Hard figures will appear in the financial data section to support any loan proposal. The objective here is to give the reader, either you or your banker, an insight into the quantitative effect of the loan on the business.

Notice that Finestkind has asked that $3,300 of the loan be reserved as a line of credit to allow the owners to take advantage of opportunities which may arise in the future. Frequently, a small business grows too fast; and, when it turns to the bank for additional financing, the funds are denied. Reserving credit insures that the funds will be available when needed but, because they are not disbursed, they will not incur additional interest expense. Finestkind is looking ahead to forestall problems, a good example of careful planning.

H. SUMMARY

The purpose of this section is to summarize the ideas you have developed in the preceding sections (see Figure 1-8). This summary will help you make sure that the different parts of the analysis make sense, that they support each other logically and coherently, and that they will leave the reader with a concise, convincing statement that the project and plan are feasible.

Figure 1-8. Sample summary statement

Finestkind Seafoods, Inc., is a fish market serving both retail and wholesale markets in and around Port Lobster, New Hampshire. Mike Gosling and Mike Swan, the owners, are seeking $36,000 to purchase the building at 123 Fish Lane, perform necessary renovations and improvements to the property, maintain cash reserves, and provide adequate working capital. This amount will be sufficient to finance transition through a planned expansion phase so the business can operate as an ongoing profitable venture.

Careful analysis of the potential market shows an unfilled demand for exceptionally fresh seafood. Mr. Gosling's local reputation will help secure a sizeable portion of the wholesale market, while Mr. Swan's managerial experience assures that the entire operation will be carefully controlled. Mr. Gosling's current studies at Pig Gut State will provide even more control over the projected growth of Finestkind and complement the advice of a carefully selected working Board of Directors.

The funds sought will result in a greater increase in fixed assets than may be shown, as Mr. Gosling will be performing much of the renovation and improvements himself. The additional reserve and working capital will enable Finestkind to substantially increase its sales while maintaining profitability.

The following checklist is an outline you can use to make sure that important points are covered in your summary. These guidelines are a suggestion. You may need to stress different points in your plan as reflected in each section. If so, make sure that they are included.

Description

1. What type is your business: primarily merchandising, manufacturing, or service? What is the product?
2. Is it a new business? A take-over? An expansion?
3. What is your business form: sole proprietorship, partnership, corporation?
4. Why will your business be profitable?
5. What hours and days will your business operate? Is it a seasonal business?
6. What have you learned about your kind of business from outside sources (trade suppliers, banks, other businesspeople, publications)?

Market

1. Who is your market?
2. How will you attract and hold your share of the market?
3. How will you satisfy your market?
4. How will you price your product?

Competition

1. Who are your nearest competitors?
2. How is their business?
3. What have you learned from their operations?

Location

1. What are your location needs?
2. What kind of building do you need?
3. Why is this a desirable area? a desirable building?

Management

1. How does your background/business experience help you in this business? Also, for your own benefit, what weaknesses do you have and how will you compensate for them? What related work experience have you had?
2. Who is on the management team?
3. What are the duties of each individual on the management team? Are these duties clearly defined? How?
4. What additional resources have you arranged to have available to help you and your business?

Personnel

1. What are your personnel needs now?
2. What will your needs be in three years?
3. Are their wages salary or hourly? Will you require overtime? Will you give fringe benefits? What about employment taxes?
4. What is your plan for training personnel for both operations and management?

Application and expected effect of loan

1. Why do you need this money?
2. How is the loan to be applied?
3. How will the loan (or other injection of new funds) make your business more profitable?

2. FINANCIAL DATA

Policy and control are the key ingredients of any successful business. Policy is the statement establishing the goals of your business. Control is measuring the accomplishment of policy goals. The heart of the operation is in the accounting system. Before you start your business, it is essential that you have a competent public accountant set up a paperwork system that will give you adequate accounting records. If you can't afford this, you are simply too undercapitalized to be in business. If you don't understand the need for this, you don't have enough management experience to be starting a business. This is a typical problem area for the vast majority of small businesses. Control is essential. If you don't control your business, it will control you.

The overriding policy of a business is to find out what the market wants, provide satisfaction of those wants, and to do so while making a profit. The implementation of your policy depends on planning and using your plan as a means of controlling your business. The first step towards managing your business for profits is to establish a bookkeeping system which provides you with the raw data for the five control documents which will be developed in this section: (1) balance sheet, (2) break-even analysis, (3) income statement, (4) cash flow, and (5) deviation analysis.

Your bookkeeping system should be simple enough for you or an employee to keep up-to-date on a daily basis with provisions made for weekly, monthly, quarterly, and yearly summaries. The system must contain cash controls; a checkbook and a tape cash register are part of your bookkeeping system. Beyond this, your method of bookkeeping should be suited to your specific needs. Since your bookkeeping system is the basis of your business information (control) system and since only you know what kind of information you will require beyond the demands of this section, no attempt is made in this handbook to set up a system for you.

There are some good bookkeeping systems available. They fall under three general categories:

1. Do-it-yourself
2. Business' service firms (consultants)
3. Accountants (public, CPA, in-house)

Each category has definite advantages and disadvantages. You should decide which suits your needs best. The do-it-yourself systems are lowest in cost but require more time and often provide less information than professional business service firms and accountants. However, business service firms and accountants do cost considerably more. Your best bet is to check out all three before making your decision. Keep in mind that business service firms and accountants can frequently act as outside staff (management consultants) for your business as part of their duties. This extra service alone might justify their higher cost.

The five control documents (balance sheet, break-even analysis, income statement, cash flow, and deviation analysis) mentioned earlier are the backbone of your planning efforts. Properly used, they act as a budgeting tool, an early-warning system, a problem-identifier, and a solution-indicator. Used inconsistently or not at all, they are worthless; used incorrectly, they are dangerous. Misleading financial information can lead to bad, often disastrous, decisions. These documents needn't be very complicated. Develop your financial statements with an eye on your information needs, using your common sense as a guide to the level of detail that is required for your business. It is possible to suffer from too much information, too. These statements are to be used systematically. Make it policy to spend at least several hours, preferably free of distraction, checking them over each month, once your business is underway. By doing so, the data will be of maximum use to you; it will help you plan your profits, make good business decisions, and set reasonable objectives for the future.

Ultimately, your accounting system should be a working model of your business. A business manager has two concurrent objectives: to make a profit and to pay bills as they come due. The balance sheet records the past effects on your business of such decisions as setting prices, purchasing or leasing new equipment, or hiring new workers. More to the point, it records what the cash position *(liquidity)* of the business is and what the owner's equity is at a given point in time: these are directly affected by the income statement and the cash flow.

The *break-even analysis* is also based on the income statement and cash flow. It is a technique that no business, no matter how tiny, can afford to ignore. Basically, a break-even analysis shows the volume of revenue from sales that is necessary to exactly balance fixed and variable expenses. This document can be used to help make information available for decision-making in areas such as setting prices, purchasing or leasing new equipment, projecting profit (or loss) at different volumes, and even in hiring a new worker.

The two main financial statements are the income statement and the cash flow. The income statement, also called the *profit and loss statement,* is designed to show changes in the owner's equity by subtracting expenses from revenue. The cash flow is designed to show how well the company is managing its cash (liquidity) by subtracting disbursements from receipts. Together, the balance sheet, break-even analysis, income statement, and cash flow afford a comprehensive model of the operations, liquidity, and the past and near future of your business. If there is only a single statement that is available, most accountants advise that it be the cash flow, since a business that can't pay its bills can't stay in business for long even though the business may be operating at a profit.

Projections or forecasts are an integral part of your financial data, and are critical to accurately evaluating the feasibility of your deal and to planning just how large an investment is required to get the business to a stable level of operation. Your assumptions must be carefully thought out and explained. Be honest here for your own benefit. Over-optimism can lead to failure.

The following items should appear in the financial data section:

A. Sources and applications of funding
B. Capital equipment list
C. Balance sheet
D. Break-even analysis
E. Pro Forma income statements
F. Pro Forma cash flow analysis
G. Deviation analysis
H. Historical Financial Reports for existing business

A. SOURCES AND APPLICATIONS OF FUNDING

This subsection must be included if your business plan will also serve as a financing proposal. It is a restatement of the information in chapter 1, "G. Application and Expected Effect of Loan or Investment." Major anticipated expenditures should be supported by copies of contracts, lease and/or purchase agreements, or similar documents and included in the supporting documents (see Figure 2-1).

Figure 2-1. Sample statement of sources and application of funding

Finestkind Seafoods, Inc.
Sources and applications of funding

Sources—Bank Loans	
Mortgage loan	$22,000
Term loan	10,700
Reserved loan	3,300
Owners' investment	5,000
Total	$41,000
Applications	
Purchase building	$22,000
Equipment	2,200
Renovations	4,000
Inventory	500
Working capital	4,000
Reserve for Contingencies	8,300
Total	$41,000

To be secured by
Assets of the Business
Signatures of the Principals
Mike Gosling
Mike Swan
SBA Guarantee

B. CAPITAL EQUIPMENT LIST

Your business plan should contain a *capital equipment list* (see Figure 2-2) to help maintain control over depreciable assets, to insure against letting your reserve for replacement of capital equipment become too low or be used as a slush fund, and to assist in the creation of a *cost budget.*[1]

Figure 2-2. Sample capital equipment list

Finestkind Seafoods, Inc.
Capital equipment list

Major Equipment and Normal Accessories	Model	*Cost or List Price (lower)
Storequip, Inc., display case, glass front, refrigerated	Handmade	$ 200
Storequip, Inc., display case, glass front, ice	SST6-77k	400
Dayton air compressor	#45-cah-990	115
Bendix standing freezer	3979-7584	125
Nameless, Inc., standard freezer		50
Cleaning table, fibreglassed	Handmade	200
Freezing locker and compressor	Handmade	3,000
Total		$4,090
Minor Shop Equipment		
Miscellaneous knives, scalers, etc.		$ 75
Miscellaneous display trays, storage boxes		50
Total		$ 125
Other Equipment		
Pickup truck with insulated body	19-- Ford, Lo-bed	$1,885
Safe	1879 Mosler	100
Cash Register	523 NCR	50
Calculator	TI-120	65
Light fixture	Custom design	100
Total		$2,200
Total Capital Equipment		$6,415

*Note: If applicable, be sure to include sales tax and installation fees.

Capital equipment is that equipment which you use to manufacture a product, provide a service, or use to sell, store, and deliver merchandise. It is not equipment which you will sell in the normal course of business. Rather, it is equipment that you will use and wear out or consume as you do business (this does not include items which are expected to need replacement annually or more frequently). Examples of capital equipment are office furniture and business machines (desks, typewriters, adding machines), store fixtures (display cases, refrigeration units, permanent fixtures such as air conditioners, lighting fixtures), machinery used to make products (lathes, presses), and vehicles utilized for deliveries. None of these items is expected to wear out before a period of years. These goods are depreciable, and their cost is expressed as "depreciation" expense on the income statement.

A sample capital equipment list for Finestkind is shown in Figure 2-2. No depreciation (accumulated) would be shown.

C. BALANCE SHEET

Balance sheets are designed to show how the assets, liabilities, and net worth of a company are distributed at a given point in time. The format (see Figure 2-3) is standardized to facil itate analysis and comparison. Do not deviate from it.

Figure 2-3. Sample balance sheet

Name of business
December 31, 19--
Balance sheet

Assets		Liabilities and net worth	
Current assets	________	Current Liabilities	________
Fixed assets	________	Long-term liabilities	________
Less accumulated depreciation	________	Total liabilities	________
Net fixed assets	________	Net worth	________
Total assets	________	Total liabilities and net worth	________
Footnotes:			

Balance sheets for all companies, great and small, contain the same categories:

1. Current assets: Cash, government securities, marketable securities, notes receivable (other than from officers or employees), accounts receivable, inventories, prepaid expenses, any other item which will or could be converted into cash in the normal course of business within one year.

[1] A *cost budget* is another useful control document which, due to the scope of this handbook, has been ommitted. Its function is to allocate indirect expense (overhead, interest on loans, etc.) to separate operations of the business on a pro rata basis. It is especially important for a business which submits bids on contract to be familiar with this procedure. The SBA has an excellent booklet on this topic (SBA Management Aid #221. Business Plan for a Small Contractor).

2. Fixed assets: Land, plant, equipment, leasehold improvements, other items which have an expected useful business life measured in years. Depreciation is applied to those fixed assets which (unlike land) will wear out. The fixed asset value of a depreciable item is shown as the net of cost minus accumulated depreciation.
3. Other assets: Intangible assets such as patents, royalty arrangements, copyrights, exclusive use contracts, notes receivable from officers and employees.
4. Current liabilities: Accounts payable, notes payable, accrued expenses (wages, salaries), taxes payable, current portion of long-term debt, other obligations coming due within the year.
5. Long-term liabilities: Mortgages, trust deeds, intermediate and long-term bank loans, equipment loans.
6. Net worth: Owner's equity, retained earnings.
7. Footnotes: You should provide displays of any extraordinary item (for example, a schedule of payables). Contingent liabilities (such as a pending lawsuit) should be included in this section.

The details will differ according to the kind of business you are in, the size of your business, and the amount of information which your accounting system makes available. This order is important and should be followed. The sub-categories are arranged in order of decreasing liquidity (for assets) and decreasing liquidity immediacy (for liabilities).

If your balance sheet is assembled by an accountant, he will specify that it was done *with* or *without audit.* If you do it yourself, it is without audit. The decision whether to use an accountant, and, if you do, to what extent, should be made carefully. This may be important for tax purposes or other legal reasons.

A sample balance sheet for Finestkind Seafoods, Inc., is given in Figure 2-4. The balance sheet for Finestkind is modestly detailed. No depreciation has been taken, for example, because the business has just been started; also, the net worth section could have been more complex. The important thing to notice is that this balance sheet provides the proper level of detail for the purposes of the principals, who jointly own all of the stock. Some financing agencies may want to see balance sheets projected for each quarter for the first year of operation and annually for the next two years. These projections show changes in debt, net worth, and the general condition of the business.

The analysis of a balance sheet is a subject beyond the focus of this text. For further advice, other than what is given below, write to the nearest Merrill, Lynch, Pierce, Fenner & Smith office for their free publication How to Read a Financial Report, or consult your library. There are many books on this subject.

Balance sheet analysis (preliminary)

1. Working capital. Working capital is calculated by subtracting *current liabilities* from *current assets. Cash* is part of *working capital.* The working capital for Finestkind is negative, a dangerous but not uncommon position for many small (and, at times, large) businesses to be in. A negative, or low, working capital position is a major danger signal. A firm with this kind of working capital position is said to be *illiquid,* or to be suffering from a *liquidity* problem. Because

Figure 2-4. Sample balance sheet for Finestkind Seafoods, Inc.

Finestkind Seafoods, Inc.
October 15, 19--
Balance sheet

Current assets:	
Cash	$ 530
Accounts receivable (net)	100
Merchandise inventory	700
Supplies	175
Prepaid expenses	80
Total current assets	$1,585
Fixed assets:	
Fixtures and leasehold improvements	$3,750
Building (freezer)	3,000
Equipment	1,100
Trucks	2,500
Total fixed assets	$10,350
Total assets	$11,935

Current liabilities:	
Accounts payable	$2,077
Current portion LTD	1,440
Total liabilities current	$3,517
Long-term liabilities:	
Notes payable (a)	$ 535
Bank loan payable (b)	1,360
Equity loan payable (c)	1,250
Total long-term liabilities	$3,145
Total liabilities	$6,662
Net worth: Owners' equity	$5,273
Total liabilities and net worth	$11,935

Accounts payable display	
Eldredge's, Inc.	$1,700
Lesswing's	119
Paxstone	180
Pig Gut Reefer	78
	$2,077

(a) Dave N. Hall for electrical work
(b) Term loan secured by '64 Jeep, '71 Ford
(c) S & C Greed Finance Corp., Pig Gut, N.H.

owners' equity is less than the debt, the creditors, in effect, "own" the business, and bankers would be reluctant to loan any more. Among possible solutions for this type of problem would be seeking more funds through long-term borrowing or through additional equity investment, selling fixed assets and leasing them back from the buyer, and finding a way to finance the *accounts payable* (perhaps by putting repayments on a monthly basis spread over a term of years.

2. Comparison. Comparison of year-end balance sheets over a period of years will highlight trends and spotlight weak areas. Since Finestkind is new, this option

is not open to them. However, they can compare their business to other, similar operations by *ratio analysis.*

3. Ratio analysis. This technique permits comparison in terms of percentages rather than dollars, thus making comparison with other companies more accurate and useful. Among more useful ratios are:
   a. Current Ratio. This measures the liquidity of a company: their ability to meet obligations coming due during the business year. It is calculated by dividing *current assets* by *current liabilities.* For Finestkind, divide $1,585 by $3,517. This yields a current ratio of 0.45, which is substantially below the rule-of-thumb 2.0 many analysts like to see. Finestkind is illiquid. However, you really need to know exactly what is represented by the figures to make a meaningful analysis (e.g., inventory composition and quality of receivables).
   b. Acid Test. This is another measure of liquidity (sometimes called the *quick ratio*), and it is calculated by dividing the most liquid assets (cash and securities and possibly accounts receivable) by current liabilities. For Finestkind, $630 ÷ $3,517 = 0.18, which is well below the 1.0 rule-of-thumb.

A word of caution: the rule-of-thumb ratios are not to be considered infallible, since the date on which the balance sheet is taken and the kind of business will affect the ratios you come up with. Some companies occasionally need a current ratio of 2.7 to be considered liquid; others need 1.5 or even less (such as department stores just prior to the Christmas rush, when their inventories are very large by trade figures and their payables particularly high). Use your judgment augmented by trade figures for your type of business. Such figures are available from your accountant, your banker, trade magazines, and other sources., e.g., *Barometer of Small Business* (Accounting Corporation of America), *Ratio Analyses for Small Business* (Small Business Administration), *Key Business Ratios* (Dunn and Bradstreet), and *Annual Statement Studies* (Robert Morris Associates) (see Appendix D). These and other reference materials should be available in your local library.

D. BREAK-EVEN ANALYSIS

A *break-even analysis* provides you with a sales objective which is expressed in either the number of dollars or units or production at which your business will be breaking even—that is, where it is neither making a profit nor losing money (Figure 2-5). If you know your break-even point, you have a definite target that you can plan to reach by carefully reasoned steps. Many businesses have destroyed themselves by ignoring the need for a break-even analysis. It is essential to remember: increased sales do not necessarily mean increased profits.

Calculating the break-even point can be simple (for a one-product business) or complex (for a multi-line business), but, whatever the complexity, the basic technique is the same. Some of the figures you need to calculate the break-even point will have to be estimates. It is a good idea to make your estimates conservative by using somewhat pessimistic sales and margin figures and by slightly overstating your expected cost figures. The basic break-even equation is:

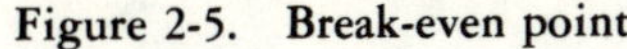

Figure 2-5. Break-even point

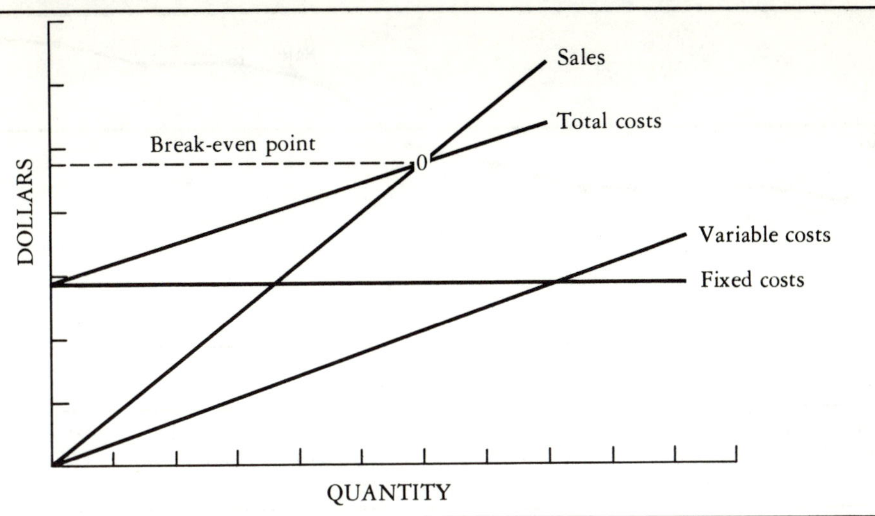

$$S = FC + VC$$

S = Break-even level of sales in dollars
FC = Fixed costs in dollars
VC = Variable costs in dollars

Fixed costs are those costs which remain constant no matter what your sales volume may be, those costs which must be met even if you make no sales at all.[2] These include overhead, such as rent, office and administrative costs, salaries, etc., and hidden costs, such as interest and depreciation. *Variable costs* are those costs associated with sales including cost of goods sold, variable labor costs, and sales commissions. (These cost figures are further developed in the next section, "Pro Forma Income Statements.")

If, instead of calculating a dollar break-even, you want to determine how many sales you need monthly to break even, you simply divide the monthly break-even derived above in dollars by the average monthly sales (see Figure 2-6).

Figure 2-6. Calculation for sales needed per month at break-even

Average unit selling price = $3.00	=	$3.00
Average customer repeat sales = 2X/Week	=	6.00
4.3 weeks/month; thus, average customer sale/month	=	25.80
Thus, customers needed at BE	=	230/month 7.6/day

[2]These costs remain constant in a relevant range. However, if at a greatly increased sales volume you need a new building, your fixed costs will rise. Refer to Figure 2-18, which indicates which types of costs are fixed and which are variable.

Figure 2-7. Break-even analysis diagram

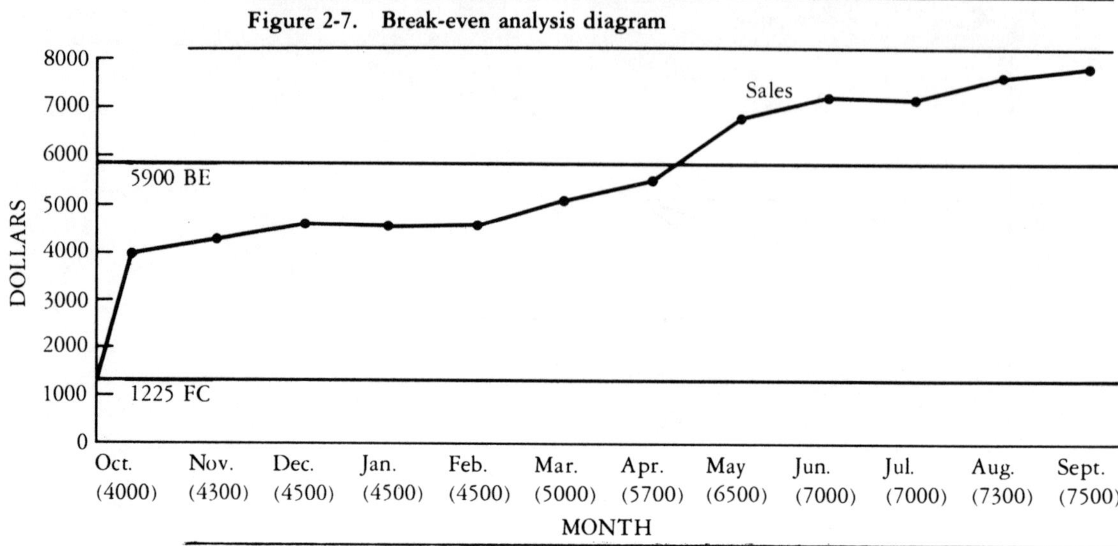

Break-even analysis also may be represented pictorially, and the diagram in Figure 2-7 helps with forecasts, budgets, and projections. Using a diagram enables you to substitute different combinations of numbers to obtain a rough estimate of their effects on your business. A helpful technique is to make worst-case, best-case, and most-probable-case assumptions, to chart them, and then derive more accurate figures by applying the formulas suggested above. This can be of special value if you are contemplating a capital investment and want a quick picture of the relative merits of buying or leasing an item. To make maximum use of your break-even analysis, utilize it in areas other than sales; you have more control over your expenditures than you do over sales.[3]

E. INCOME PROJECTIONS
(Pro forma income statements[4])

Income statements, also called *profit and loss statements,* are complementary to balance sheets. The balance sheet gives a static picture of the company at a given point in time. An income statement provides a moving picture of the company during a particular period of time. Income statements that are cast into the future are called *income projections.* Income projections are forecasting and budgeting tools estimating income and anticipating expenses in the near to middle range future. For most small businesses, income projections covering the next three years are adequate.

You do not need a crystal ball to make your projections. While no set of predictions will be 100 percent accurate, experience and practice tend to make your projections more precise. Even if your projections are not accurate, they will provide you with a set of bench-

[3]Break-even analysis can be directly applied to profit-planning by modifying the basic formula S = FC + VC. The formula for this calculation is: S = FC + VC + P. Here, P stands for Profit. Suppose you wish to determine the volume of sales at which you will make a particular profit. Using P = S – FC – VC, you will be able to figure the amount of sales you need.

[4]Pro forma simply means "projected." It represents what the business is expected to look like at some specified time in the future.

marks to test your progress toward short-term goals. They become your budget.

There is nothing sacred about income projections. If they are not exact, correct them to make a more realistic guide. However, at what point you should do this is a matter for your judgment. Do not change your predictions more than quarterly or even semi-annually. In a short period, certain trends will be magnified, and these distortions will usually even out in the long run. Of course, if you omit a major-expense item or a new source of revenue, you ought to make immediate corrections, but use your common sense. The reasoning behind income projection is: since most expenses are predictable and income usually doesn't fluctuate drastically, the future will be much like the past. If, for example, your gross margin has historically been 30 percent of net sales, it will, unless there is strong evidence to the contrary, continue to be 30 percent of net sales. If you are in a start-up situation, you can find income ratios for businesses similar to yours in the publications listed in Appendix D. This will improve the accuracy of your financial forecast.

It is important to be systematic and thorough when you list your expenses. The expense that makes your business illiquid is often one which is overlooked, and therefore, not planned for. There are some expenses that simply cannot be foreseen, and the best way to allow for them is to be conservative in your estimates and to document your assumptions. Try to understate slightly your expected sales and overstate your expected expenses. It is far better to exceed a conservative projection than to budget optimistically and then fall below the projected margins. However, being too far under can also create problems, such as not having adequate cash to finance growth. Basing income projections on hopes is a frequent cause of business failure. Be realistic. Your budget is intimately tied to your forecasted sales and expense figures.

Income statements and projections are standardized to facilitate comparison and analysis (Figure 2-8). They must be dated to indicate the period of time they cover and should also contain notes to explain any unusual items such as windfall profits, litigation expense and judgments, changed in depreciation schedules, and so forth.

The information given in each category is explained as follows:

Net sales: (*Gross sales* less returns and allowances).
Cost of goods sold: Includes cost of inventories.
Gross margin (Gross sales minus *cost of goods sold):* Represents the gross profit on sales without taking indirect costs into account.
Operating expense: These are the costs (when added to *other expense*) which must be met no matter what the sales level is. The order in which they are stated is not so important. Thoroughness is. If some costs are trivial, lump them together under a heading of *miscellaneous* but be prepared to break them out if the *miscellaneous* category becomes more than an arbitrary 1% of *gross sales.*
Other expense: These are non-operating expenses. The most common is Interest expense. It is helpful to have the Interest expense prominently displayed to highlight the cost of money.
Total expense: Sum of *operation expense* and *other expense.*
Profit (loss) pre-tax (Gross margin minus *total expense):* This is the tax base, the figure on which your tax is calculated.
Taxes: Consult your accountant.
Net profit (loss) (profit (loss) pre-tax minus *taxes):* This represents the success or lack thereof for your business. There are two ways to make this figure more positive: increase sales and/or decrease expenses.

For the most useful projection: state your assumptions clearly. Do not put down numbers that you cannot rationally substantiate. Do not puff your *gross sales* figures to make the *net profit* figure positive. Give yourself conservative *sales* figures and a pessimistic *expense* figure to make the success of your deal more probable. Be realistic.

Any assumptions you make must be footnoted. You should review them at least once a quarter, or more frequently, to check their validity and, if necessary, to make adjustments. As a budget tool, a comparison of the actual progress of the business against the projections should be done on a monthly basis. You need to detect deviations as soon as possible so that you can correct problems before they become disasters.

Figure 2-8. Sample format for pro forma income statement

Finestkind Seafoods, Inc.
Pro Forma Income Statement
October 15, 19- to October 14, 19-

Net sales	________	
Less: Cost of goods sold	________	
Gross margin	________	
Operating expense		
Salaries and wages		________
Payroll taxes and benefits		________
Rent		________
Utilities		________
Maintenance		________
Office supplies		________
Postage		________
Automobile and truck		________
Maintenance delivery equipment		________
Insurance		________
Legal and accounting		________
Depreciation		________
Other		________
Operating expense total	========	
Other expense		
Interest payments		________
Other expense total	========	
Total expense	========	
Profit (loss) pre-tax	________	
Taxes	________	
Net profit (loss)	========	

Smaller businesses, for both planning purposes and for loan proposal requirements, should project for three years. The proper sequence of income-projection pages in your business plan would be as follows:

1. Three-year summary. See Figure 2-9 for sample.

2. First year projected by month. See Figure 2-10 for sample. If the business does not break even in the first year, continue projections by month until it does.
3. Years 2 and 3 (if not included in monthly projections, step 2) projected by quarter. See Figure 2-11 for sample.
4. Notes of explanation. See Figure 2-12 for sample.

Figure 2-9. Sample three-year summary of income projection

Finestkind Seafoods, Inc.
Pro Forma Profit & Loss
Three-Year Summary

	Year 1	Year 2	Year 3
Sales			
Wholesale	$27,400	$68,800	$84,000
Retail	40,400	91,000	91,000
Total sales	67,800	159,800	175,000
Cost of material	52,884	124,625	136,550
Variable labor cost	900	3,250	5,200
Cost of goods sold	53,784	127,875	141,750
Gross margin	14,016	31,925	33,250
Operating expenses			
Utilities	1,200	1,680	1,920
Salaries	5,160	14,400	16,000
Payroll taxes and benefits	480	1,360	1,520
Advertising	480	720	720
Office supplies	120	180	180
Insurance	600	600	600
Maintenance and cleaning	240	300	300
Legal and accounting	504	740	740
Delivery expense	1,320	1,802	1,764
Licenses	60	60	60
Boxes, paper, etc.	120	240	240
Telephone	600	720	720
Depreciation	480	480	480
Miscellaneous	276	400	400
Total operating expense	11,640	23,682	25,644
Other expenses:			
Interest (mortgage) 9.75%	2,160	2,160	2,160
Interest (loan) 10.75%	900	900	900
Total other expenses	3,060	3,060	3,060
Total expenses	14,700	26,742	28,704
Net Profit (loss) pre-tax	$(684)	$5,183	$4,546*

*Net profit is down slightly because of an increase in salaries paid to the two partners.

Figure 2-10. Sample pro forma profit and loss statement detailed by month for first year

Income Projections
Finestkind Seafoods, Inc.
October 19-- to September 19--

	Oct. 19-	Nov. 19-	Dec. 19-	Jan. 19-	Feb. 19-	Mar. 19-	Apr. 19-	May 19-	June 19-	July 19-	Aug. 19-	Sept. 19-	Total
Sales													
Wholesale	1,000	1,200	1,400	1,600	1,800	2,200	2,400	2,800	3,100	3,100	3,300	3,500	27,400
Retail	3,000	3,100	3,100	2,900	2,700	2,800	3,300	3,700	3,900	3,900	4,000	4,000	40,400
Total sales	4,000	4,300	4,500	4,500	4,500	5,000	5,700	6,500	7,000	7,000	7,300	7,500	67,800
Cost of material	3,120	3,354	3,510	3,510	3,510	3,900	4,446	5,070	5,460	5,460	5,694	5,850	52,884
Variable labor cost								200	200	200	200	100	900
Cost of goods sold	3,120	3,354	3,510	3,510	3,510	3,900	4,446	5,270	5,660	5,660	5,894	5,950	53,784
Gross margin	880	946	990	990	990	1,100	1,254	1,230	1,340	1,340	1,406	1,550	14,016
Operating expenses													
Utilities	100	100	100	100	100	100	100	100	100	100	100	100	1,200
Salaries	430	430	430	430	430	430	430	430	430	430	430	430	5,160
Payroll taxes and benefits	40	40	40	40	40	40	40	40	40	40	40	40	480
Advertising	40	40	40	40	40	40	40	40	40	40	40	40	480
Office supplies	10	10	10	10	10	10	10	10	10	10	10	10	120
Insurance	50	50	50	50	50	50	50	50	50	50	50	50	600
Maintenance and cleaning	20	20	20	20	20	20	20	20	20	20	20	20	240
Legal and accounting	42	42	42	42	42	42	42	42	42	42	42	42	504
Delivery expense	110	110	110	110	110	110	110	110	110	110	110	110	1,320
Licenses	5	5	5	5	5	5	5	5	5	5	5	5	60
Boxes, paper, etc.	10	10	10	10	10	10	10	10	10	10	10	10	120
Telephone	50	50	50	50	50	50	50	50	50	50	50	50	600
Depreciation	40	40	40	40	40	40	40	40	40	40	40	40	480
Miscellaneous	23	23	23	23	23	23	23	23	23	23	23	23	276
Total operating expense	970	970	970	970	970	970	970	970	970	970	970	970	11,640
Other expenses:													
Interest (mortgage) 9.75%	180	180	180	180	180	180	180	180	180	180	180	180	2,160
Interest (loan) 10.75%	75	75	75	75	75	75	75	75	75	75	75	75	900
Total other expenses	255	255	255	255	255	255	255	255	255	255	255	255	3,060
Total all expenses	1,225	1,225	1,225	1,225	1,225	1,225	1,225	1,225	1,225	1,225	1,225	1,225	14,700
Net profit (loss) pre-tax	(345)	(279)	(235)	(235)	(235)	(125)	29	5	115	115	181	325	(684)
Taxes	—	—	—	—	—	—	—	—	—	—	—	—	—
Net profit (loss)	—	—	—	—	—	—	—	—	—	—	—	—	—

Figure 2-11. Sample pro forma profit and loss statement detailed by quarter for second and third years

Income Projections
Finestkind Seafoods, Inc.
By Quarters, Years 2 and 3

	1st qtr Year 2 (Dec)	2nd qtr Year 2 (Mar)	3rd qtr Year 2 (Jun)	4th qtr Year 2 (Sept)	Total Year 2	1st qtr Year 3 (Dec)	2nd qtr Year 3 (Mar)	3rd qtr Year 3 (Jun)	4th qtr Year 3 (Sept)	Total Year 3
Sales										
Wholesale	14,800	16,000	18,000	20,000	68,800	18,000	20,000	22,000	24,000	84,000
Retail	21,000	21,000	22,000	27,000	91,000	21,000	21,000	22,000	27,000	91,000
Total sales	35,800	37,000	40,000	47,000	159,800	39,000	41,000	44,000	51,000	175,000
Cost of material	27,925	28,850	31,200	36,650	124,625	30,450	32,000	34,300	39,800	136,550
Variable labor cost	750	750	750	1,000	3,250	1,000	1,200	1,500	1,500	5,200
Cost of goods sold	28,675	29,600	31,950	37,650	127,875	31,450	33,200	35,800	41,300	141,750
Gross margin	7,125	7,400	8,050	9,350	31,925	7,550	7,800	8,200	9,700	33,250
Operating expenses										
Utilities	420	420	420	420	1,680	480	480	480	480	1,920
Salaries	3,600	3,600	3,600	3,600	14,400	4,000	4,000	4,000	4,000	16,000
Payroll taxes and benefits	340	340	340	340	1,360	380	380	380	380	1,520
Advertising	180	180	180	180	720	180	180	180	180	720
Office supplies	45	45	45	45	180	45	45	45	45	180
Insurance	150	150	150	150	600	150	150	150	150	600
Maintenance and cleaning	75	75	75	75	300	75	75	75	75	300
Legal and accounting	185	185	185	185	740	185	185	185	185	740
Delivery expense	387	420	471	524	1,802	378	420	462	504	1,764
Licenses	15	15	15	15	60	15	15	15	15	60
Boxes, paper, etc.	60	60	60	60	240	60	60	60	60	240
Telephone	180	180	180	180	720	180	180	180	180	720
Depreciation	120	120	120	120	480	120	120	120	120	480
Miscellaneous	100	100	100	100	400	100	100	100	100	400
Total operating expense	5,857	5,890	5,941	5,994	23,682	6,348	6,390	6,432	6,474	25,644
Other expenses:										
Interest (mortgage)	540	540	540	540	2,160	540	540	540	540	2,160
Interest (loan)	225	225	225	225	900	225	225	225	225	900
Total other expenses	765	765	765	765	3,060	765	765	765	765	3,060
Total all expenses	6,622	6,655	6,706	6,759	26,742	7,113	7,155	7,197	7,239	28,704
Net profit (loss) pre-tax	440	715	1,365	2,665	5,183	437	645	1,003	2,461	4,546
Taxes	—	—	—	—	—	—	—	—	—	—
Net profit (loss)	—	—	—	—	—	—	—	—	—	—

Figure 2-12. Sample notes of explanation for Finestkind Seafoods, Inc., income projections

1. Sales: Includes sales of seafood and sales of ancillary products (seasonings, sauces, bait-bags, bait).
2. Finestkind plans to service the wholesale trade more extensively than is shown here, although the trend has been built into the projection. Retail sales are expected to be more volatile than wholesale, leveling off at a capacity of $9,000/month due to space restrictions. The volatility is due to seasonal traffic, which builds up from late March to the late summer peak. The increase shown in item 2, wholesale, are based on both the greater number of restaurants open in the summer and the intensive effort planned for the winter months, to sell directly to the many restaurants to which Finestkind has not yet introduced its product. Sales for September 19-- were $5,450; so these figures are very conservative.
3. Cost of material: Finestkind's inventory has an average cost of 70 percent of sales (including a start-up spoilage rate of 5 percent which has been reduced to under 1 percent of sales), and has been calculated as 78 percent of sales to allow for the fluctuation of dockside fish prices during the winter.
4. Variable labor cost: One part-time counter helper for summer weekends and one part-time cutter to help prepare seafood for restaurant trade at peak times.
5. Utilities: Prorated by agreement with the utility companies involved. The expected prorated figure is $90/month, but it may increase.
6. Salaries: $50/week for each principal. This is an extremely low figure to which the principals have agreed in order to build up their business.
7. Payroll taxes and benefits: 9.5 percent of Salaries.
8. Advertising: Local newspaper and radio spots. It is believed that a consistent, though modest, campaign will be more productive than a sporadically intensive campaign.
9. Insurance: Includes liability, key-man disability, and life.
10. Maintenance and cleaning: Mainly supplies. A market such as this must meet stringent health codes.
11. Legal and accounting: Retainers to Mason Petrocelli, J. D. and Scrooge Farley, CPA.
12. Delivery expense: Delivery of merchandise to restaurants and other markets. Year 2 delivery expenses computed at 2.62 percent of wholesale sales. Year 3 delivery expenses computed at 2.10 percent of wholesale sales. As the wholesale business increases, it is anticipated that route efficiency will also increase, causing delivery expenses to decrease.
13. Licenses: Required by state and municipality.
14. Boxes, paper, etc.: Packaging supplies.
15. Telephone: Needed for sales, pricing, contacting both suppliers and market.
16. Depreciation: Accountant's figures for depreciation of plant and equipment.
17. Miscellaneous: Operating expenses too small to be itemized.
18. Interest (mortgage): $22,000 at 9.75 percent for fifteen years.
19. Interest (loan): $8,500 at 10.75 percent for seven years.

If you are already in business or are considering taking over an existing business, historical statements (income statements and balance sheets) should be included for two previous years. Tax returns help to substantiate the validity of unaudited statements.

The following interpretations of items in the income projections will explain how the figures on the projection were calculated and detail the assumptions which were made.

Numerical references have been made by line (e.g., 19. *Maintenance and cleaning*).

1. Sales: Includes sales of seafood and sales of ancillary products (seasonings, sauces, baitbags, bait).

2. & 3. Finestkind plans to service the wholesale trade more extensively than is shown here, although the trend has been built into the projection. Retail sales are expected to be more volatile than wholesale, leveling off at a capacity of $9,000/month due to space restrictions. The volatility is due to seasonal traffic, which builds up from late March to the late summer peak. The increase shown in (2) Wholesale are based on both the greater number of restaurants open in the summer and the intensive effort planned for the winter months, to sell directly to the many restaurants to which Finestkind has not yet introduced their product. Sales for September 19- were $5,450; so these figures are very conservative (perhaps more than they should be, but the degree of pessimism is a matter of judgment). Too much pessimism is also bad. It can distort a reasonable profit picture and a reasonable deal may then appear infeasible.

4. *Total:* Sales is the sum of items 2 and 3.

5. *Cost of Material:* Finestkind's inventory has an average cost of 70 percent of sales (including a start-up spoilage rate of five percent which has been reduced to under 1 percent of sales), and has been calculated at 78 percent of sales to allow for the fluctuation of dockside fish prices during the winter.

7. *Variable labor cost:* One part-time counter helper for summer weekends and one part-time cutter to help prepare seafood for restaurant trade at peak times.

8. *Cost of goods sold:* Sum of items 6 and 7.

10. *Gross margin:* Item 4 minus 8.

13. *Utilities:* Prorated by agreement with the utility companies involved. The expected prorated figure is $90/month, but it may (probably will) increase.

14. *Salaries:* $50/week for each principal. This is an extremely low figure to which the principals have agreed in order to build up their business. This is a direct result of being undercapitalized.

15. *Payroll taxes and benefits:* 9.5 percent of item 14.

16. *Advertising:* Local newspaper and radio spots. This is an expense which they might profitably increase. They think (correctly) that a consistent, though modest, campaign will be more productive than a sporadically intensive campaign.

18. *Insurance:* Includes liability, key-man disability and life.

19. *Maintenance and cleaning:* Mainly suppliers. A market such as theirs must meet stringent health codes.

20. *Legal and accounting:* Retainers to Mason Petrocelli, Esq. and Scrooge Farley, CPA.

21. *Delivery expense:* Delivery of merchandise to restaurants and other markets. Year 2 delivery expenses computed at 2.62 percent of wholesale sales. Year 3 delivery expenses computed at 2.10 percent of wholesale sales. As the wholesale business increases, it is anticipated that route efficiency will also increase, causing delivery expenses to decrease.

22. *Licenses:* Required by state and municipality.
23. *Boxes, paper, etc.:* Packaging supplies.
24. *Telephone:* Needed for sales, pricing, contacting both suppliers and market.
25. *Depreciation:* Accountant's figure for depreciation of plant and equipment. This is perhaps too low.
26. *Miscellaneous:* Operating expenses too small to be itemized.
27. *Total: operating expense:* Sum of items 13 through 25.
29. *Other expenses:* Non-operating costs broken out to give them special prominence.
30. *Interest (mortgage):* $22,000 at 9.75 percent for fifteen years.
31. *Interest (loan):* $8,500 at 10.75 percent for seven years.
33. *Total: other expenses:* Sum of items 30 and 31.
35. *Total: all expenses:* Sum of items 27 and 33.
37. *Net profit (loss) pre-tax:* Item 10 minus 35.
    No further items because no tax due.

Finestkind does not expect to make much money for the first two years of operation. For a business of this kind, particularly for one so severely undercapitalized, this is no surprise. Even if it were well capitalized with no debt at all, the net profit would have been only $3,000 for the year.

This is a projection based on conservative figures. Actually in their more optimistic plan for the year, Gosling and Swan expect to have total fixed costs of $1,100/month, not the $1,225 projected, and sales figures 12.5 percent higher. Their budgeted net profit should be $2,680, not the projected net loss of $684. If their margin were to continue at 30 percent of sales, not the 22 percent projected, their net profit for the year would be $8,783, the "best case" assumption.

One item conspicuously absent is rent. On the *cash flow* this appears as mortgage ($250/month). Another item that is missing is loan amortization, which also appears on the cash flow ($145/month). These represent an added $140/month for debt retirement, which is not an expense item since it is for capital improvements which will be written off as depreciation expense over the course of several years. It is important not to double-deduct expenses. Such a practice is not only illegal but also obscures the information on the operation of your business. Information is the most valuable result of financial statements.

The content as shown in the samples may have to be modified to fit your particular operation, but do not change the basic form. Remember, the purpose of financial statements and forecasts is to provide you with a maximum amount of usable information, not to dazzle a prospective investor.

F. PRO FORMA CASH FLOW

The *cash flow* is the most critical planning tool for a new or growing business. Businesses need cash for start-up or growth. The cash flow analysis shows: (1) how much cash will be needed, (2) when it will be needed, and (3) where it will come from. A schematic model of

Figure 2-13. Schematic model of cash flow

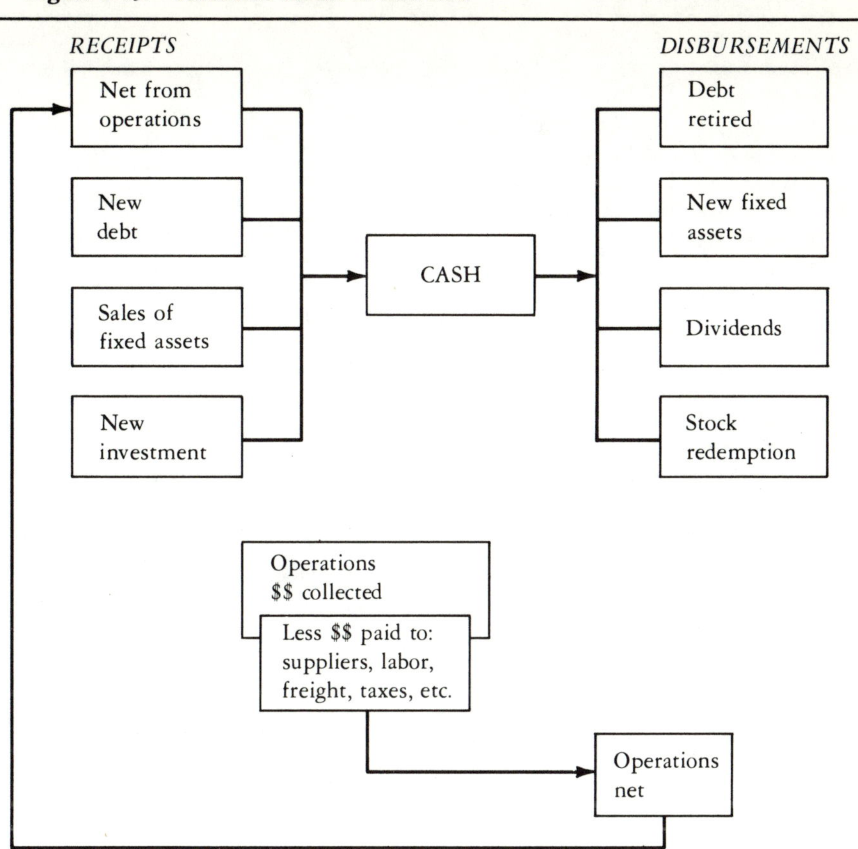

the cash flow is shown in Figure 2-13. Remember: cash in-flows must equal or be greater than cash out-flows.

The cash flow attempts to budget the cash needs of a business and shows the flow of cash into and out of the business over a period of time. Cash flows into the business from sales, collection of receivables, capital injections, etc., and flows out through cash payments for expenses (Figure 2-14). This financial tool emphasizes the points in the calendar when money will be coming into and going out of the business. The advantage of knowing when cash outlays will be made is the ability to plan for those outlays without being forced to resort to unexpected borrowing to fulfill cash needs. By constructing a cash flow for the near-to-intermediate future, you can see the effect of a loan on your business more clearly than you can from an income statement. Often, you can find ways to finance your business operations or to borrow only a specific amount which will help keep your interest expense as low as possible.

Cash is generated primarily by sales. However, not all sales are *cash* sales. Perhaps this does not apply in your business, but, if you offer any credit (charge accounts, term pay-

Figure 2-14. Cash flow

Cash at beginning of period
Add revenues
2. Sales of products to be collected currently
3. Cash to be received from other sources
4. Cash received from prior period sales
5. Cash received from assets sold
6. Cash received from equity investment
7. Cash received from loans
8. Cash from bad debts recovered
9. Miscellaneous cash received

Total cash received

Subtract expenses
10. New inventory purchased
11. Salaries/wages to be paid
12. Fringe benefits to be paid
13. New equipment to be purchased
    14. processing equipment
    15. office, sales equipment
    16. transportation equipment
17. Insurance
18. Fees
    19. accounting
    20. legal
21. Utilities
    22. telephone
    23. heat, light, power
24. Advertising
25. Principal and interest on debt
26. Transportation
    27. oil, gas
    28. vehicle maintenance
    29. tires
30. Freight
31. Provision for bad debts
32. Taxes to be paid
    33. income (state, federal)
    34. property/excise
    35. payroll
    36. sales
37. Dividends to be paid
38. Provision for unforeseen contingency

Total expenses
Cash at end of period

ments, trade credit, etc.) to your customers, you may want to have a means of telling when your sales turn into cash-in-hand. Unlike the income projection, the cash flow can indicate this. Your business may be subject to some seasonal bills, and, again, a cash flow makes the liquidity problems attending such large, occasional expenses clear.

A cash flow deals only with actual cash transactions. Depreciation, a noncash expense, does not appear on a cash flow. Loan repayments (including interest), on the other hand, do appear, since they represent a cash disbursement.

After it has been developed, the cash flow should be used as a budget. If the expenses for a given item increase over the amount allotted for a given month, you should find out why and take corrective action as soon as possible; if the figure is less, then also find out why. By reviewing the movement of your cash position you can better control your business. If expenses are lower than anticipated, it is not necessarily a good sign; it may be that a bill wasn't paid. On the other hand, the lowered expense may alert you to a new way of economizing. Discrepancies between expected expenses and revenues and the actual flow of cash often indicate problem areas. If the sales figures don't follow the cash flow, look for the cause. Perhaps the projections are too low. Your cash flow is not a universal cure which will make your job as manager or owner superfluous. It is a tool which you must use and use consistently.

The next section deals with deviation analysis and takes a more formal approach to using a budget. It uses the cash flow and income statement as self-correcting signals. If,

Figure 2-15. Sample pro forma cash flow* detailed by month for first year

Finestkind Seafoods, Inc.
October 19-- to September 19--

		Oct. 19-	Nov. 19-	Dec. 19-	Jan. 19-	Feb. 19-	Mar. 19-	Apr. 19-	May 19-	June 19-	July 19-	Aug. 19-	Sept. 19-	Total
Cash receipts														
Income from sales														
Wholesale		1,000	1,200	1,400	1,600	1,800	2,200	2,400	2,800	3,100	3,100	3,300	3,500	27,400
Retail		3,000	3,100	3,100	2,900	2,700	2,800	3,300	3,700	3,900	3,900	4,000	4,000	40,400
Total cash receipts		4,000	4,300	4,500	4,500	4,500	5,000	5,700	6,500	7,000	7,000	7,300	7,500	67,800
Cash disbursements														
Cost of goods		3,120	3,354	3,510	3,510	3,510	3,900	4,446	5,070	5,460	5,460	5,694	5,850	52,884
Variable labor									200	200	200	200	100	900
Advertising		100	25	25	25	25	40	40	40	40	40	40	40	480
Insurance				150			150			150			150	600
Legal and accounting			125			125			125			125		500
Delivery expense		80	85	90	95	100	110	110	120	130	130	135	135	1,320
Fixed cash disbursements		688	688	688	688	688	688	688	688	688	688	688	688	8,256
Loan #1		145	145	145	145	145	145	145	145	145	145	145	145	1,740
Mortgage		250	250	250	250	250	250	250	250	250	250	250	250	3,000
Total cash disbursements		4,383	4,672	4,858	4,713	4,843	5,283	5,679	6,638	7,063	6,913	7,277	7,358	69,680
Net cash flow		(383)	(372)	(358)	(213)	(343)	(283)	21	(138)	(63)	87	23	142	(1,880)
Cumulative cash flow		(383)	(755)	(1,113)	(1,326)	(1,669)	(1,952)	(1,931)	(2,069)	(2,132)	(2,045)	(2,022)	(1,880)	
Fixed cash disbursements														
Utilities	100													
Salaries	430													
Payroll taxes and benefits	40													
Office supplies	10													
Maintenance and cleaning	20													
Licenses	5													
Boxes, paper, etc.	10													
Telephone	50													
Miscellaneous	23													
	688													
Cash on hand: Loan proc.		4,000												
Cash		535												
Opening balance		4,535	4,152	3,780	3,422	3,209	2,866	2,583	2,604	2,466	2,403	2,490	2,513	
Plus cash receipts		4,000	4,300	4,500	4,500	4,500	5,000	5,700	6,500	7,000	7,000	7,300	7,500	
Less cash disbursements		4,383	4,672	4,858	4,713	4,843	5,283	5,679	6,638	7,063	6,913	7,277	7,358	
Total new balance		4,152	3,780	3,422	3,209	2,866	2,583	2,604	2,466	2,403	2,490	2,513	2,655	

*Assuming $8,500 loan and $22,000 mortgage loan.

Figure 2-16. Sample pro forma cash flow detailed by quarter for second and third years

Finestkind Seafoods, Inc.
By Quarters for Years 2 and 3

	1st qtr Year 2 (Dec)	2nd qtr Year 2 (Mar)	3rd qtr Year 2 (Jun)	4th qtr Year 2 (Sept)	Total Year 2	1st qtr Year 3 (Dec)	2nd qtr Year 3 (Mar)	3rd qtr Year 3 (Jun)	4th qtr Year 3 (Sept)	Total Year 3
Cash receipts										
Income from sales										
Wholesale	14,800	16,000	18,000	20,000	68,800	18,000	20,000	22,000	24,000	84,000
Retail	21,000	21,000	22,000	27,000	91,000	21,000	21,000	22,000	27,000	91,000
Total cash receipts	35,800	37,000	40,000	47,000	159,800	39,000	41,000	44,000	51,000	175,000
Cash disbursements										
Cost of goods	27,925	28,850	31,200	36,650	124,625	30,450	32,000	34,300	39,800	136,550
Variable labor	750	750	750	1,000	3,250	1,000	1,200	1,500	1,500	5,200
Advertising	180	180	180	180	720	180	180	180	180	720
Insurance	150	150	150	150	600	150	150	150	150	600
Legal and accounting	185	185	185	185	740	185	185	185	185	740
Delivery expense	387	420	471	524	1,802	378	420	462	504	1,764
Fixed cash disbursements	4,772	4,805	4,856	4,909	19,342	5,263	5,305	5,347	5,389	21,304
Loan #1	435	435	435	435	1,740	435	435	435	435	1,740
Mortgage	750	750	750	750	3,000	750	750	750	750	3,000
Total cash disbursements	35,534	36,525	38,977	44,783	155,819	38,791	40,625	43,309	48,893	171,618
Net cash flow	266	475	1,023	2,217	3,981	209	375	691	2,107	3,382
Cumulative cash flow	266	741	1,764	3,981			584	1,275	3,382	

Fixed cash disbursements	Year 2	Year 3
Utilities	140	160
Salaries	1200	1333
Payroll taxes and benefits	113	126
Office supplies	15	15
Maintenance and cleaning	25	25
Licenses	5	5
Boxes, paper, etc.	20	20
Telephone	60	60
Miscellaneous	33	33
Total fixed cash disbursements	4835	5335

over a three-month or six-month period, your projections are seriously off, take the time to understand the differences *before* changing them. This is one reason for documenting your assumptions in projections even though you may be the only person to see them. Then make new projections to set more realistic goals for the company.

In contrast to balance sheets and income statements, there is no standardized form to follow in devising a cash flow. One form frequently used by bankers and analysts is prepared by Robert Morris Associates. A useful format which tends to serve the information needs of bankers and analysts as well as—and most importantly—the business itself is shown in Figures 2-15, 2-16, and 2-17.

Figure 2-17. Sample notes of explanation for pro forma cash flow

Notes of Explanation
for
Finestkind Seafoods, Inc., Pro Forma Cash Flow

1. Wholesale: See income projection for derivation of these figures.
2. Retail: See income projection for derivation of these figures.
3. Cost of goods: 78 percent of line 5.
4. Variable labor: $200/month from May to mid-September to handle the extra tourist traffic on weekends and extra seafood preparation costs associated with two restaurants which do weekend clambakes during peak season.
5. Advertising: $100 for initial burst, $25/month thereafter.
6. Insurance: Payable quarterly.
7. Legal and accounting: Retainers payable quarterly.
8. Delivery expense: Projected to increase less slowly than wholesale sales due to careful route planning.
9. Loan #1: $8,500 SBA guaranteed loan at 10.75 percent for seven years.
10. Mortgage: $22,000 at 9.75 percent for fifteen years.

For financing purposes, cash flow analysis (see chapter 5) is more important than any other single aspect of financial management. Bankers and other outside financing intermediaries will almost always look for a cash flow analysis in preference to any other financial statement.

The only receipts shown on this cash flow are from sales. *Loan proceeds* are shown on line 36 in the cash balance reconciliation (Figure 2-15). This data sheet shows how business operations affect the cash flow. Since most purchases of inventory are made on a cash basis (cash or 10-day net), the principals of Finestkind plan to have a minimum of $2500 available to provide liquidity and to purchase additional equipment if needed. Otherwise, line 41 showing the new balance is only used as a quick check on whether they are following their budget or not.

References in the following explanations are to line numbers on the accounting sheet (Figure 2-15) unless otherwise noted.

3. *Wholesale:* See income projection (Figure 2-8) for derivation of these figures.
4. *Retail:* See income projection (Figure 2-8) for derivation of these figures.
8. *Cost of goods:* 78 percent of line 5.
9. *Variable labor:* $200/month from May to mid-September to handle the extra tourist traffic on weekends and extra seafood preparation costs associated with two restaurants which do weekend clambakes during peak season.
10. *Advertising:* $100 for initial burst, $25/month thereafter.
11. *Insurance:* Payable quarterly.
12. *Legal and accounting:* Retainers payable quarterly.
13. *Delivery expense:* Projected to increase less slowly than wholesale sales as a result of careful route planning.
14. *Fixed cash disbursements:* Cash expenses which do not vary with sales. See lines 25 through 35 for detail.
16. *Loan #1:* $8500 SBA guaranteed loan at 10.75 percent for seven years.
17. *Mortgage:* $22,000 at 9.75 percent for fifteen years.
19. *Total cash disbursements:* Sum of lines 8 through 17.
21. *Net cash flow:* Line 5 minus line 19.
23. *Cumulative cash flow:* This sums up the net cash flow (NCF) on a monthly basis, adding the current month NCF to the previous month's CCF. (This is useful on a periodic basis: quarterly, semi-annually, and annually, for instance. Over a longer period of time, it is of academic interest only. Some experts suggest pushing a cash flow until the cumulative cash flow becomes positive.

36. through 41. *Cash balance reconciliation:* Includes proceeds of loan less capital expenditures (see page 68 for detail). Line 38 plus line 39 minus line 40 yields the new balance (41) which becomes the opening balance (38) for the next month.

Further explanation of these items appears on the notes accompanying the income projection (Figure 2-12).

G. DEVIATION ANALYSIS

For most small businesses, the pro forma cash flow for one year provides an operating budget. You may wish to break down some of the expense items (disbursements) more finely to insure greater control, but the cash flow is a basic framework for your budget. *Budget deviation analysis* (BDA) is a direct control on your business. It can help you minimize expenses and increase profits at a time cost of approximately one evening per month. It is an essential part of your business planning effort and should not be ignored even when things are going well.

Budget deviation analysis must be performed periodically, at least on a monthly basis, if it is to be effective. If you are engaged in a business with several concurrent projects, it may be more helpful to devise separate budgets and deviation analyses for each project on a monthly basis. Budget deviation analysis provides one of the most valuable sources of current information available to you, and it is a task no manager can afford to let slide. If done properly, it will tell you at a glance which parts of your business are going out of control and which are exceeding expectations.

The budget deviation analysis form shown in Figures 2-18 and 2-19 should be modified to suit the particular needs of your business. Columns C and D are derived from

Figure 2-18. Budget deviation analysis form

Budget Deviation Analysis
Profit and Loss
Month: ___________

	A Actual For Month	B Budget For Month	C Deviation B-A	D % Deviation $\frac{C}{B}$ x 100
Sales				
Deduct: Cost of goods				
Gross profit on sales				
Operating expenses				
Variable expenses				
Sales salaries (commissions)				
Advertising				
Miscellaneous variable				
Total variable expense				
Fixed expenses				
Utilities				
Salaries				
Payroll taxes and benefits				
Office supplies				
Insurance				
Maintenance and cleaning				
Legal and accounting				
Delivery				
Licenses				
Boxes, paper, etc.				
Telephone				
Miscellaneous				
Depreciation				
Interest				
Total fixed expense				
Total expense				
Net profit				
Tax expense				
Net profit after taxes				

Figure 2-19. Budget deviation analysis of cash flow

Budget Deviation Analysis
Cash Flow
Month: ___________

	A Actual For Month	B Budget For Month	C Deviation B-A	D % Deviation $\frac{C}{B} \times 100$
Beginning cash balance				
Add: Sales revenue				
Other revenue				
Total available cash				
Deduct: Estimated disbursements				
Cost of materials				
Variable labor				
Advertising				
Insurance				
Legal and accounting				
Delivery				
Equipment*				
Loan payments				
Mortgage payment				
Property tax expense				
Deduct: Fixed cash disbursements				
Utilities				
Salaries				
Payroll taxes and benefits				
Office supplies				
Maintenance and cleaning				
Licenses				
Boxes, paper, etc.				
Telephone				
Miscellaneous				
Total disbursements				
Ending cash balance				

*Equipment expense represents actual expenditures made for purchase of equipment.

actual and budgeted figures. Experience will teach which deviations and what magnitude of deviation are significant. Any deviation, whether positive or negative, should be carefully examined, and the reasons for its existence should be understood. Next, corrective action should be taken. Suppose, for example, "utilities," budgeted for $100 in January, cost $140. The indicated action might seem to be to cut utilities expenses as soon as possible. However that month, the weather was exceptionally cold; action taken was to

Figure 2-20. Year-to-date budget deviation analysis for cash flow

Budget Deviation Analysis
Cash Flow
Year to Date: __________

	A Actual Year to Date	B Budget Year to Date	C Deviation B-A	D % Deviation $\frac{C}{B}$ x 100
Beginning cash balance				
Add: Sales revenue				
Other revenue				
Total available cash				
Deduct: Estimated disbursements				
Cost of materials				
Variable labor				
Advertising				
Insurance				
Legal and accounting				
Delivery				
Equipment*				
Loan payments				
Mortgage payment				
Property tax expense				
Deduct: Fixed cash disbursements				
Utilities				
Salaries				
Payroll taxes and benefits				
Office supplies				
Maintenance and cleaning				
Licenses				
Boxes, paper, etc.				
Telephone				
Miscellaneous				
Total disbursements				
Ending cash balance				

Calculations: A: *Add* current month actual to last month's year-to-date analysis.
B: *Add* current month budget to last month's year-to-date analysis.

*Equipment expense represents actual expenditures made for purchase of equipment.

install insulation near the end of the month, and replace a broken skylight on 1 February. If close attention had not been paid to the utilities bill, an additional loss could have

Figure 2-21. Yeat-to-date budget deviation analysis

Budget Deviation Analysis
Profit and Loss
Year to Date: ____________

	A Year to Date	B Budget to Date	C Deviation B-A	D % Deviation $\frac{C}{B} \times 100$
Sales				
Deduct: Cost of goods				
Gross profit on sales				
Operating expenses:				
Variable expenses				
Sales salaries (commissions)				
Advertising				
Miscellaneous variable				
Total variable expense				
Fixed expenses				
Utilities				
Salaries				
Payroll taxes and benefits				
Office supplies				
Insurance				
Maintenance and cleaning				
Legal and accounting				
Delivery				
Licenses				
Boxes, paper, etc.				
Telephone				
Miscellaneous				
Depreciation				
Interest				
Other				
Total fixed expense				
Total expense				
Net profit				
Tax expense				
Net profit after taxes				

Calculations: A: *Add* current month actual to last month's year-to-date analysis.
B: *Add* current month budget to last month's year-to-date analysis.

quickly teached disastrous proportions. Again, suppose sales were $5400 in January, not the anticipated $4500. The question that should have been raised here was, what did you do right? Your careful attention to a positive deviation might pay off in greatly increased profits.

Year-to-date budget deviation analysis shown in Figure 2-20 and 2-21 is another instrument of financial control. If more expenditures fall in one month than were expected, you will often find a corresponding lowering of expenditures for the preceding or following month. The year-to-date BDA helps to level out these swings. Used with the monthly BDAs, this form will save you some unnecessary arithmetic and worry as well as check the accuracy and effectiveness of your projections. With experience, your budgeting will become more exact, affording you even greater control over your business and enhancing your profitability.

As in the case with the other control documents, you should adapt the suggested formats which follow to your own particular needs. Your accountant (if you have one) can help here, but you must be the one to decide what information will be reflected by the budget deviation analyses. As mentioned in the discussion of the financing proposal, deviational analysis is not needed by your banker under most circumstances.

H. HISTORICAL FINANCIAL REPORTS

An integral part of your business plan is a record of what has happened in the immediate past. For most business deals, balance sheets and income statements for the past three years are sufficient, though it may be necessary to go further back if you are trying to raise venture capital. The third major component of your past financial condition report is your tax statement. Since this must be filed on at least an annual basis, it provides a summary of what you earned, how you earned it, and what your deductible expenses were. If you decide to sell your business, these tax reports will be the first substantiation of your asking price that will be requested.

If you do not have an accountant, you can go directly to the nearest IRS office at a time well in advance of payment day and go over your business records with a representative. By doing so, you will have the benefit of free advice from experts and may even qualify for a pre-audit of your return, which can save you trouble later. The IRS will also help you set up a record keeping system to minimize the problems of preparing your tax forms. The IRS agents are more concerned with helping businesses properly handle their financial responsibilities (taxes) than with catching those who do not. Helping businesses simply makes their job easier. If you don't have these financial records, or if you have lied to minimize your tax liabilities, you have only cheated yourself. In the first instance, you have only demonstrated your incompetence. In the second case, you have simply lowered the performance level of the business, thus making it a worse risk for a lender. Either way, it just isn't worth it.

Finally, tax records can be used as an additional source of data. For example, exact copies of wage and deduction statements are helpful in preparing projections for the future. Financial data from the past is an important planning aid.

SUMMARY

Budgeting, balancing objectives with reality, and then guiding the business to achieve the goals within the budget constraints are the real tests of management ability.

With the exception of the historical financial reports, which reflect past managerial decisions, the financial data section of your business plan stresses the importance of making careful assumptions about the objectives of your business as the first step in preparing your financial documents. These documents, particularly the income and cash flow projections, give you the basis for your planning efforts. They set up a systematic range of objectives to be met of which the break-even point is the most critical, and, through deviation analysis, they establish your principal control system, a system which will serve as an early-warning network when consistently used and which will contain built-in suggestions for remedying weaknesses in your operation. The financial records discussed in this chapter are not intended to be straitjackets. They are meant to free you from the number one problem most small business owners/managers face: how do you find time for planning when there are so manya brushfires to be put out? Your single most important asset is your time, and, to make the most effective use of your time, early planning is not a luxury; it is a necessity.

It cannot be overstressed that your control over your business is only as strong as the decisions on which those controls are based. You *must* take the time to think your business objectives through and in careful detail. You *must* make your assumptions as clear and as well defined as possible. And you *must* be prepared to review and reevaluate constantly those assumptions and to make appropriate corrections to your projections on a periodic basis.

Financial data is the heart of your planning efforts once the business has been fully articulated. The financial documents should provide you with the information to manage your business, and that information should be timely—not a month too late—to avert a full-blown problem. Solve problems before they occur, not after. This requires that you set aside time to review the information your system provides. Budget your time as well as the activities of the business. An excellent practice followed by many managers is to set aside one afternoon or evening a week away from the office and telephone for planning and review. If you have the feeling that you cannot afford the time, you have the clearest indication that you must plan, that you must take the time now. One leading bank executive would like to engrave the following advice in the minds of all businesspeople: planning is the key to business success.

3. SUPPORTING DOCUMENTS

In this section, you will want to include any documents which lend support to statements you have made in the body of the business plan. Items included here will vary according to the needs and stage of development of your particular business. The following list suggests some things which might be included:

1. Resumes (See Figure 3-1.)

Figure 3-1. Sample of functional resumes

Mike Swan

March 19- - June 19-: Line foreman, Fatback Fishfoods, East Machias, Maine. Responsible for hiring, training and directing operations of fifteen persons in Frozen Food Filleting Department. Rescheduled work flow with resultant 30 percent increase in output per worker. Implemented new purchasing system which reduced spoilage 8 percent. Reduced personnel turnovers by working with local union for revision of company contract policy and by shifting from production line to team task approach. Received Grandiose Foodstuff, Inc., award for line management and was given special assignment in September, 19-, to explain these changes to other line foremen at all twenty-two Fatback Fishfoods plants in New England and the Middle Atlantic states.

Mike Gosling

August 19- - September 19-: Self-employed carpenter. Responsibilities included cash flow forecasting, budgeting, and various other management functions needed in the operation of a single employee business. Concurrently, night courses have been taken in small business management and sales at Pig Gut State. Currently serving on the Port Lobster Zoning Board. Prior experience included a three-year term in the U.S. Navy. Married, two children.

---

2. Credit information (See forms included in appendix E.)
3. Quotes or estimates (See Figure 3-2.)
4. Letters of intent from prospective customers (See Figures 3-3 and 3-4.)
5. Letters of support from creditable people who know you
6. Leases or buy/sell agreements
7. Legal documents relevant to the business
8. Census/demographic data (See Figure 3-5.)
9. Plan of proposed or current business site (See Figure 3-6.)

Figure 3-2. Quote of estimate

WASHINGTON LICENSE 1000 MARYLAND LICENSE 2000 VIRGINIA LICENSE 3000

JOHNSON'S PLUMBING, INC.

Telephone 202/333-2222 1327 Varnum Street, Washington, D.C.

Finestkind Seafoods, Inc.
123 Fish Lane Attn: Mr. Mike Gosling September 18,19-
Port Lobster, NH 03899

Dear Mr. Smith

For the sum of $4000.00 we propose to furnish and install the plumbing and heat work as shown on your outline sketch.

All work will be guaranteed and serviced for one year from the date of completion.

Terms, We would require a down payment of $1,150.00, another payment of $1,150 when the rough plumbing and heating is completed. The balance is due upon final completion.

If the above meets with your approval, please sign and return one copy.

Signed by

Date

Thank you,

D. L. Johnson

Derek LaMont Johnson

Figure 3-3. Letter of recommendation

NIGHTLIFE CLAMBAKES
222 Rural Lane
Pig Gut & Port Lobster

September 10, 19-

Gentlemen:

It is a pleasure to write this letter of recommendation for Finestkind Seafoods, Inc. Our dealings with Messrs. Gosling and Swan have been completely satisfactory. Our business requires a dependable supply of fresh fish, clams, and lobsters of first quality. We have consistently received seafood products from Finestkind which meet these standards.

Our business is growing and we look forward to an ongoing relationship with Finestkind to satisfy our needs and customers.

Yours,

DONALD DUCK

Donald Duck

Figure 3-4. Letter of recommendation

GRANDiose Superettes

BANGOR PORTLAND YORK PORT LOBSTER

October 13, 19-

To Whom It May Concern:

We feel that it has been a privilege to do business with Finestkind Seafoods, Inc., throughout the relatively short time that they have been in existence. We perceive a strong demand for quality fresh fish and have been unable to secure the freshness and quality we desire on a regular basis from suppliers other than Finestkind.

Finestkind has been providing the quality/freshness level we require on a consistent basis. As long as they maintain their high standards, we will be pleased to continue our business with them.

Sincerely yours,

Michael Smart

Michael Smart
President

MS:ss

Figure 3-5. General characteristics of the population: 1970

General Characteristics of the Population: 1970

Census Tracts	SMSA
RACE	
All persons	**113 408**
White	112 266
Negro	821
Percent Negro	0.7
AGE BY SEX	
Male, all ages	**55 573**
Under 5 years	6 136
3 and 4 years	2 676
5 to 9 years	7 293
5 years	1 435
6 years	1 440
10 to 14 years	7 123
14 years	1 352
15 to 19 years	5 036
15 years	1 247
16 years	1 204
17 years	1 109
18 years	851
19 years	625
20 to 24 years	2 797
20 years	551
21 years	526
25 to 34 years	7 074
35 to 44 years	7 112
45 to 54 years	5 935
55 to 59 years	2 132
60 to 64 years	1 620
65 to 74 years	2 068
75 years and over	1 247
Female, all ages	**57 835**
Under 5 years	5 849
3 and 4 years	2 530
5 to 9 years	7 086
5 years	1 397
6 years	1 404
10 to 14 years	6 671
14 years	1 212
15 to 19 years	4 955
15 years	1 211
16 years	1 172
17 years	1 083
18 years	814
19 years	675
20 to 24 years	3 103
20 years	582
21 years	532
25 to 34 years	7 774
35 to 44 years	7 097
45 to 54 years	6 096
55 to 59 years	2 213
60 to 64 years	1 932
65 to 74 years	2 896
75 years and over	2 163
RELATIONSHIP TO HEAD OF HOUSEHOLD	
All persons	**113 408**
In households	112 270
Head of household	30 616
Head of family	26 930
Primary individual	3 686
Wife of head	24 214
Other relative of head	56 373
Not related to head	1 067
In group quarters	1 138
Persons per household	3.67
TYPE OF FAMILY AND NUMBER OF OWN CHILDREN	
All families	**26 930**
With own children under 18 years	17 535
Number of children	45 625
Husband-wife families	**24 214**
With own children under 18 years	16 236
Number of children	42 503
Percent of total under 18 years	90.1
Families with other male head	**516**
With own children under 18 years	150
Number of children	317
Families with female head	**2 200**
With own children under 18 years	1 149
Number of children	2 805
Percent of total under 18 years	5.9
Persons under 18 years	47 184
MARITAL STATUS	
Male, 14 years old and over	**36 373**
Single	9 822
Married	25 166
Separated	312
Widowed	861
Divorced	524
Female, 14 years old and over	**39 441**
Single	8 997
Married	25 465
Separated	560
Widowed	3 973
Divorced	1 006

Figure 3-6. Finestkind Seafoods, Inc. — layout

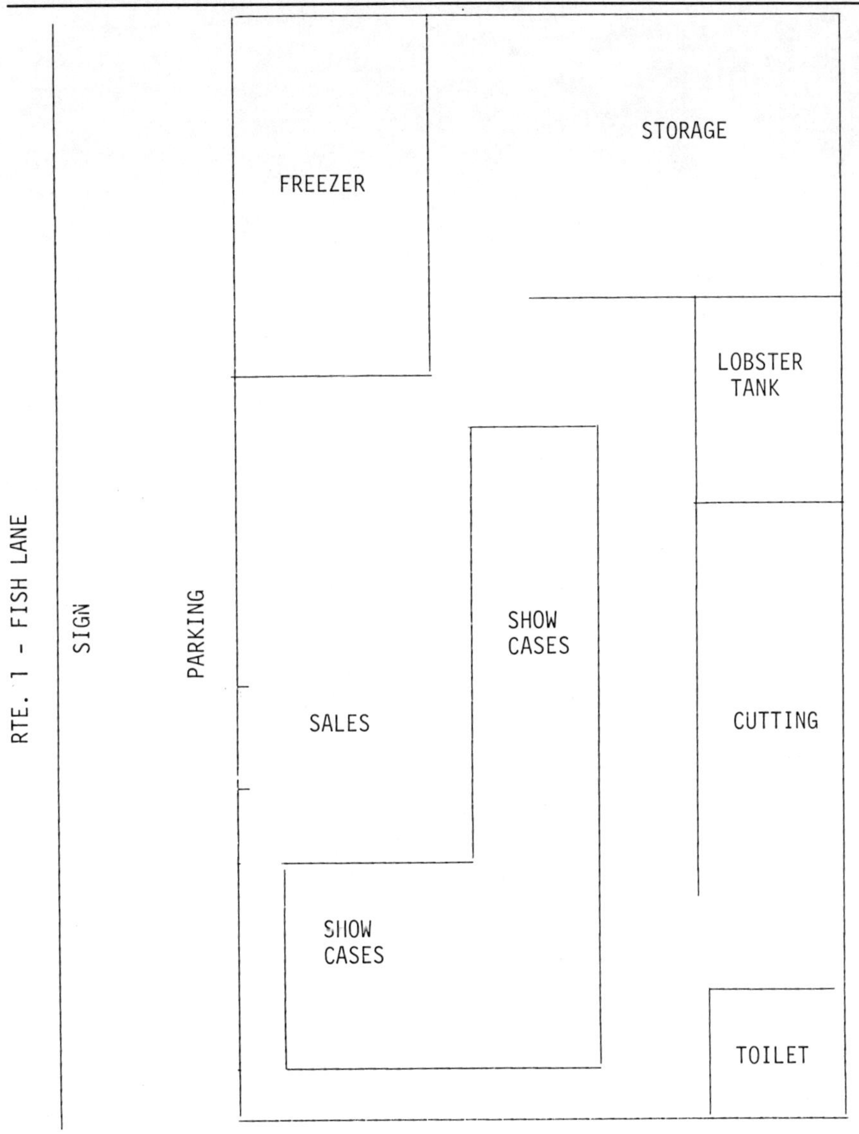

— LAYOUT —
FINESTKIND
SEAFOODS
INC.

Part II.
FINANCING GUIDE

4. FORECASTING

WHY FORECAST?

Forecasts or projections are an integral part of the financial data section of any business plan, and are actually the core or the heart of the business planning process itself. As planning tools, they are intended to be a rough map of the business's future. Projections are never 100 percent correct, but, of course, a rough map in unfamiliar territory is far better than none. If the assumptions on which the projections are based are realistic, this rough map will be accurate enough to locate prominent hazards and to establish direction for the business to follow.

Carefully done, forecasts can be used to plan for profit. Large companies spend millions of dollars forecasting, both for profit and, what may be even more important, for setting meaningful planning objectives. These objectives then become the basis for strategies the companies can use to meet their profit targets.

Forecasts anticipate what is likely to happen in the future and give you the basis for developing a plan to make the most of where you are headed. Forecasting is also useful as a means of managing change, as a way of evaluating business practices (both as a review and, with deviation analysis, as a control) and as an inexpensive means of figuring out how different practices and assumptions will affect your company.

Forecasting and constructive review are inseparable parts of the same process. The advantages of careful forecasting are many and outweigh the time, effort, and difficulty in preparing them. In fact, time spent in planning and control can save much more time than would be spent later in reacting to and trying to solve problems that could have been avoided in the first place. Thus, the forecasting process, if the assumptions are rigidly scrutinized, will pay off in preventing problems, finding better ways to operate, and sparking new ideas and deeper understandings of your business, all of which lead to stability, growth, and improved profits.

HOW TO FORECAST: THE SEVEN STEPS

Forecasting often seems like a very mysterious process. Obviously, no one can know for sure what is going to happen in the future. It is possible, though, to make reasonably accurate predictions based on a logical assessment of the facts that are available to you now. There is no magic to it, no crystal ball. There is, instead, a careful analysis of past and current business practices, a degree of extrapolation of current trends (sales, expenses, major economic shifts such as inflation, and others), and a great deal of creative examination, evaluation, and revision of the assumptions you use to operate your business.

Forecasting provides you with an excellent opportunity to determine how your business operates. This opportunity will seem rare if you are as pressed for thinking time as most people are. Rare as it may be, you can and must create it. You will simply have to force yourself to invest this time towards a smoother, more profitable operation in the future.

The following process is designed to show some ways to make forecasts as accurate and therefore as useful as possible. The test which should be applied to this process is one of reasonableness. The secret is simple enough. It is a matter of continually reexamining the assumptions that are being used to make sure that they make sense. However, like many things which are simple in theory, it is not that simple in practice, and so the following process has been developed to make reexamining assumptions more understandable and more useful for people who are not experts in doing this kind of work.

Seven Steps of Forecasting

1. Identify all fixed and variable costs.
2. Make your break-even analysis: determine your break-even point, the level of sales necessary to cover all of your expenses.
3. Evaluate the odds of reaching the break-even level.
4. Determine when you will reach break-even.
5. Consider your downside risk: plot the break-even level on a graph against two curves, reasonable growth and pessimistic growth.
6. Translate the graphs into income forecasts.
7. Translate the income forecasts into a cash flow.

The following sections discuss each of these steps in detail and provide illustrations of the different techniques you will need to use in creating your own forecasts for your own business. If you have problems at any point, and it is reasonable to expect that you may, do not hesitate to contact your local business information center, your accountant, your banker, or someone else who can help you find the answers.

Step 1: Identify all fixed and variable costs.

As a going concern, your business will generate expenses over the course of a year. Once all of the potential expenses that the business will incur have been identified, they must be classified as either "fixed" or "variable." *Fixed costs, as the name implies, are those costs or expenses which are expected to remain relatively constant over a reasonable period of time.* They are unaffected by changes in output or sales up to the point where the level of operation reaches the capacity of the existing facilities. At that point, major changes would have to be made, such as the expansion of existing plant and equipment or the construction of new facilities. Such actions would increase the fixed costs. However, under normal operating conditions, the fixed costs (also referred to as indirect costs, overhead, or burden) will remain constant.

Those costs which vary or change directly with output are *variable costs* or expenses. These are the costs which are associated with production and/or selling and are frequently identified as "costs of goods sold." As compared with fixed costs, which continue whether the firm is doing business or not, variable costs do not exist if the firm is not doing business. Thus, by definition, variable costs are zero when no output is being produced. At that time, fixed costs are the only costs which will be incurred.

Examples of Fixed and Variable Costs

Fixed costs	*Variable costs*
Depreciation of plant and equipment	Cost of goods sold
	Factory labor
Rent, mortgage payments	Sales commissions
Interest	Materials inventory
Executive and office salaries	Freight-in (and -out)
General office expenses	Variable factory expenses
Property taxes	Direct labor
	Sales expenses

As you review the cost items for the past year or more, keep in mind that they fluctuate seasonally and that each item must have a reason. These expenses must individually and/or jointly serve a business purpose. If they do not, then why incur them? Question each cost category to see if it can be reasonably lowered or, perhaps, increased. Advertising, for example, is frequently underfunded to the detriment of the business. By examining these costs one by one, you will reap several benefits. Among these will be added understanding of where all of the money is dribbling away, ideas for economies, or perhaps warnings of coming problems.

For most businesses, a lot of helpful information is available. If you are involved in a start-up or in an expansion, or even if you are in a stable, ongoing business situation and are trying to make your operation more efficient, there are various sources of help. Your accountant, because he is familiar with the cost structures of a variety of different businesses, will be able to help you make sure you have identified all of the expenses you can reasonably expect. In addition, various publications, such as the *Barometer of Small Business* (Accounting Corporation of America) and the *Annual Statement Studies* (Robert Morris Associates), show average operating expenses for a wide range of small businesses across the country. Other pamphlets and publications, such as the Bank of America's *Small Business Reporter Series,* The U.S. Department of Commerce's *Urban Business Profile Series,* and different booklets from the Small Business Administration, deal with the specific problems encountered in different kinds of businesses, and will provide average operating data for ventures similar to yours. Reference information on these and other materials is included in appendix D.

These publications and others can be extremely helpful. If you are projecting costs which differ significantly from the trade averages, double-check your assumptions. If you are projecting costs which are significantly lower than the averages, really force yourself to determine if these expectations are valid or if they are just hopeful figments of your imagination. If you continue to project expenses which differ from the trade averages, try to differ on the side of caution by either slightly overstating expenses or putting any borderline items into the fixed expense category. Prudence and profit seem to go together.

Step 2: Make your break-even analysis.

Your break-even analysis is helpful in more than forecasting. It is also an important problem-solving tool. Break-even analysis can be invaluable for determining whether to buy or lease, whether to expand into a new area, whether to build a new plant, and for many other decisions. Break-even analysis will not force a decision, of course, but it will provide you with additional insights into the effects of important business decisions on the bottom line. Informed decisions have a much better chance of being correct than random seat-of-the-pants decisions.

Break-even also shows the impact on your business of changing your price structure. As the price goes down and your gross margin goes down, break-even shoots up, usually very rapidly.

Simply stated, *break-even refers to the level of sales necessary to cover all of the fixed costs and variable costs.* If a firm's costs were all variable, the problem of break-even would never arise because sales would automatically cover the costs of goods sold as long as you priced each item or service at cost or above. By having some fixed as well as variable costs or expenses, the firm must suffer losses up to a given volume. We look for the point where the gross profit or excess of selling price over cost exactly equals the fixed expenses. The break-even is the point at which the business neither makes a profit nor has a loss. At that point, the business "breaks even."

Break-even analysis will provide a sales objective which can be expressed in either a number of dollars or a number of units of production or sales or whatever else is relevant to show the level at which the business will be breaking even. If the break-even point is known, it can be a definite target to be reached and exceeded by carefully reasoned steps. Many businesses have destroyed themselves by ignoring the need for break-even analysis. It is essential to remember that increased sales do not necessarily mean increased profit. For example, if the selling price is reduced in order to stimulate sales, the break-even point may be forced upwards to such an extent that, practically speaking, the business could never achieve sufficient sales to break even.

Break-even is a planning tool, a decision-making tool, a pricing tool, and an expense control tool. As a planning tool, break-even analysis indicates the targets the business must achieve and provides a quick and direct way of evaluating the impact of the various alternatives on the business strategy. If the break-even is unrealistically high, then it is clear that the business will never be able to achieve those levels of sales because it would require an inordinately high percentage of the target market, or it would require the processing of more goods and services than the business has the capacity to handle, and so, clearly, that alternative should not be pursued. On the other hand, if the break-even is extremely low, it may suggest that a more profitable strategy could be pursued or at least seriously considered.

These considerations lead to the second function of break-even. As a decision-making tool, break-even helps to evaluate the various alternatives that are available to the business. Following these alternatives through a break-even analysis is a far safer way of determining their impact on the business than actually experimenting with the real operation. An anticipation of the negative impact of certain alternatives will automatically help to eliminate those alternatives and thereby avoid their impact. Problem solving by avoidance is far preferable to any other alternative that may be available to a business.

Break-even is an important pricing tool, showing the relationship between price, contribution, and volume. These factors are related to the decision-making aspect of break-even analysis as it provides a direct and straightforward approach to considering a series of prices and their impact on the business. It is generally assumed that as price goes down, volume is likely to increase. As noted, however, this is not necessarily desirable. The underlying focus must be on the relationship between contribution or gross profit and fixed costs. This is critical, because, as the contribution or gross profit decreases relative to the fixed costs, the break-even point will increase. It may increase to such a point that the sales figures required for break-even are simply too high, thereby creating a totally unrealistic situation.

Finally, as an expense control tool, break-even provides a way of evaluating the impact on the business of various expenses and provides an interesting and sometimes very different way to consider the need or relevance of a given expense on the total operation. If it is not essential and the business is feasible without it, it can be eliminated and profits improved. If it is essential but forces an unrealistically high break-even, then the choice must be made not to pursue that course of action.

There is a very simple and very direct relationship between expenses, sales, and profit. Profit can be increased typically by increasing sales or decreasing expenses. Accordingly, it is useful for any business to inspect expenses as profits which would otherwise be available to the owners and, on that basis, determine whether or not particular expenses are truly essential to the business operation. An ongoing break-even analysis can be incorporated as part of the expense review and control process together with careful observation of the relationship between sales, gross profits (gross margin), and expenses, to maintain a floating sales objective. Expenses have a tendency to increase almost invisibly in most operations. Accordingly, the owners of these operations may feel that they are improving or doing better, and yet find their profits are, in fact, shrinking. An ongoing break-even analysis will help to indicate the impact of these changes on the total business operation.

Break-even is based on the relationship of fixed and variable costs to sales.

Let FC = Total fixed costs in dollars
S = Total sales as 100 percent
VC = Total variable costs as a percentage of sales

Break-even = FC ÷ (S – VC)/100

For example, assume that an appliance dealer has fixed costs (FC) of $70,000, sales of $1,000,000 per year, and variable costs (VC) of $650,000.

Break-even = $70,000 ÷ (100% -- 65%)/100
= $70,000 ÷ (35%)/100
= $200,000

In other words, the dealer needs $200,000 per year in sales to cover alal of the fixed expenses. At this point, the business will make neither a profit or a loss—the business will "break even." The appliance industry has a high margin, whereas, for example, the grocery business has a low margin, 15% as opposed to 35%. For the same fixed expenses, a grocer would need $70,000 ÷ 15%, or $467,000 in sales. The lower the contribution margin, the higher the sales must be to cover the same amount of fixed costs.

To calculate a projected break-even, when you do not know what your total VC will be, it is necessary to use a variation of the S × FC + VC formula. If you know what *gross margin* (profit on sales) you expect as a percent of sales, the following formula can be used (Figure 4-1):

GM = Gross margin as a % of sales
BE = FC ÷ GM

With this type of analysis, it becomes relatively simple to evaluate the impact of discrete units of cost. Do you really need a fancy office or a Lear jet (fixed expenses)? Each decision here can be evaluated in terms of the impact of that expense on the break-even level of sales. A gross profit or mathematical approach to break-even provides for a very rapid calculation of the impact of any of these changes. You could experiment, for example, with adding specific expense categories and quickly calculating the changed break-even point which would represent the impact of that particular strategic decision.

Break-even for a multiple product line can be calculated for any given product-mix by looking at the average contribution for the total product line. It can be calculated for the individual products as well. However, practically speaking, you would need to calculate the break-even for every combination of alternatives. This would become unworkable simply because of the large number of calculations involved. A useful alternative is a graphic representation. Representing break-even analysis by using a break-even chart is helpful for many people because they can quickly see the differences the changes in this decision-making would make on the break-even level in the business.

One helpful technique is to make worst-case, best-case and most-probable-case assumptions, to chart them, and then derive more accurate figures by applying numerical formulas as previously suggested. For example, this can be of special value in considering a capital investment where the need is for a quick picture of the relative merits of buying or leasing an item. Finally, to make maximum use of break-even analysis, the results can be focused on expense categories rather than sales. Expense categories typically are subject to much greater control than sales. It is possible to reduce sales by merely deciding not to make commitments in expense categories. However, increasing sales involves the decisions about other categories that are not so directly controlled.

The break-even chart is constructed on a per unit basis as shown in Figure 4-2. In

Figure 4-2. Break-even chart

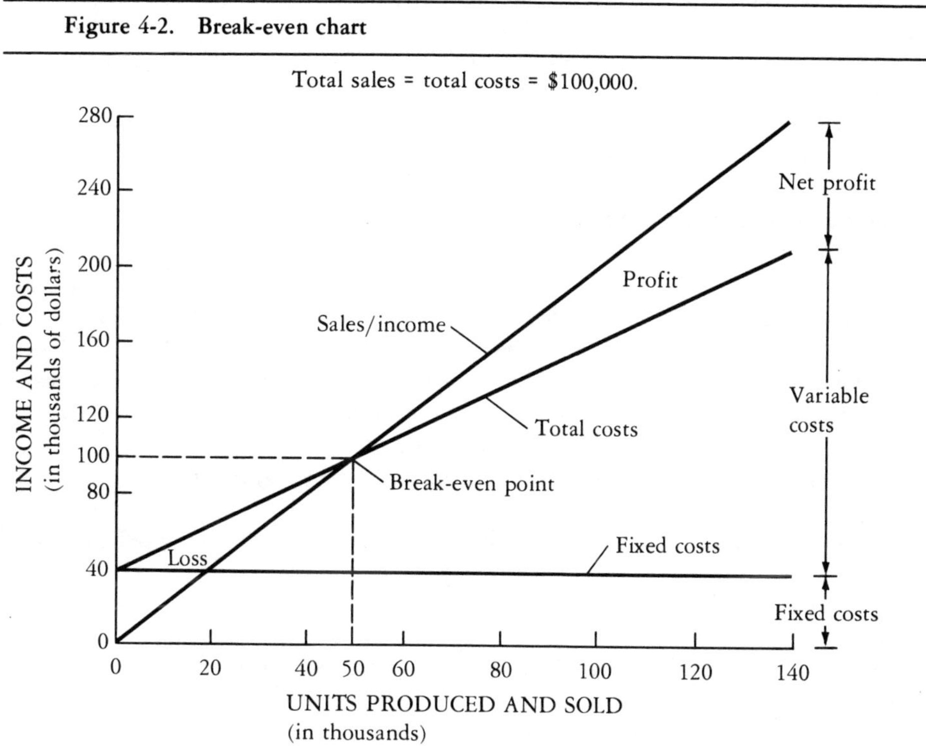

the diagram (Figure 4-2), fixed costs of $40,000 are represented by a horizontal line, and variable costs of $1.20 per unit by a vertical line rising from the fixed point. Sales are figured at $2.00 per unit, and it is assumed that each unit produced is sold. (This may not be especially accurate in the short run, but in the long run it is a perfectly reasonable assumption.) The sales/income line will start from the origin or the zero point. Since the rate of ascent of the sales/income line is greater than that of the variable costs, the two lines will eventually cross. The break-even point is where they coincide. In Figure 4-2, this is 50,000 units.

You should keep in mind that this is a linear chart based on a constant selling price. By changing the assumptions, you can quickly use this chart to your advantage. For example, you can estimate the effect of price changes fairly precisely by varying the slope of the income line. Similarly, by altering the slope of the variable costs line, you can approximate cost changes. Once you have experimented some with the possibilities here, you will probably find this to be a very interesting, thought-provoking exercise.

It is frequently helpful to calculate the cash break-even point for a business as well as the profit and loss break-even point. There are two important reasons for this. Some of the items contained in the profit-and-loss (income) statement are not cash items—depreciation, for example. Also, for a given period of time, some sales may be in the form of receivables, and thus the actual receipts of funds will lag behind the technical date of the sale. The extent to which receivables lag behind payables will introduce potential cash flow problems for the firm. If there are important differences between sales and cash flow, you may want to construct a break-even chart for each.

Step 3: Evaluate the odds of reaching break-even.

Once you have determined the level of sales you must reach before you make a profit, then you need to determine the feasibility of this target. What are the odds of reaching this break-even? One way to test this is to convert the gross dollar sales needed for break-even into some other unit which can then be compared against the capacity of the business or the size of the market (Figure 4-3). If the break-even occurs at or near the capacity of the business, or if your analysis shows that you must capture all or more than all of the available target market, the feasibility of the deal is suspect. The odds of business success are loaded against you. Clearly, this is a subjective process, but then, so is the rest of forecasting. It is not possible to eliminate this subjectivity completely. The purpose here is to try to make these evaluations as reasonable as possible.

Suppose you own a soup restaurant. If so, how many bowls of soup does break-even represent? How many per working day? Per hour? How does that fit your capacity? Does it mean a larger number of tables, a lesser number, more waiters? Are the numbers feasible?

By putting the numbers into more concrete images, you may find the criterion of reasonableness (feasibility) easier to use. A business is an interconnected system with each part related to all other parts. This is why piecemeal solutions often merely shift the problem to another area of the business operation. If you are aware of how the parts interrelate, you have a great advantage over those in your competition who are not, and the unaware are the great majority.

As noted, another way of using your break-even analysis is to consider what share of the target market your break-even represents. While defining your target market is extremely difficult, it is very important. The effort you put into defining that target (and continually redefining it, nothing remains unchanged) will pay giant dividends.

This is a critical step in determining the feasibility of your deal. If you can't say that your business makes sense at this point (as an expansion needing 110 percent of the market, for example), then reexamine your plan. The process of reexamination may make you aware of new solutions. In any case, recognizing limitations through this type of analysis

Figure 4-3. Sample break-even feasibility analysis

Break-even Feasibility Analysis
Consideration of Satellite Operation

	Boston	Atlanta
Variable costs	%	%
1. Operator commissions	55	50
Supplies	12	12
2. Manager commission	5	10
Total variable costs	72	72
Gross profit	28	28
Fixed costs	$	$
3. Salon manager	10,400	10,400
Employment taxes and benefits	1,000	1,000
4. Rent	5,500	9,000
Travel	1,200	1,200
Utilities	1,200	1,200
Advertising	1,200	1,200
Telephone and answering service	600	1,000
Insurance	600	600
Legal and accounting	1,200	1,200
Property taxes and licenses	300	300
Repairs and maintenance	500	200
5. Depreciation	3,600	2,500
6. Interest	1,600	7,475
Miscellaneous	600	600
Total fixed costs	$29,500	$37,875
Break-even = $\frac{tfc}{gp\%}$	105,357	135,270
BE/Quarter	26,339	33,820
BE/Month	8,780	11,273
BE/Week	2,026	2,820

Feasibility Analysis

	Boston	Atlanta
I. Required operators:		
Commissions earned at $200/week		
Operators required for BE	5.57	7
Actual and planned operators	6	8—10
II. Required customers:		
Average revenue/customer—$15		
Per week (6-day operation)	135	
Customers/operator/hour	1	
Operator/capacity/hour, average	2	

III. Required customers, annual:
1. Average revenue per visit—$15
2. Average customer visits salon every six weeks or 8.6 times per year
3. Annual average expenditure per customer—$130
4. Break-even requirements for Atlanta 135.270
5. Number customers required $\frac{135.270}{(130)}$ = 1,041 customers

is much cheaper than charging blindly into a disaster. If it isn't going to work at all, acknowledge it at this point and save yourself the agony of failure.

Step 4: Determine when you will reach break-even.

As in the other steps, you are making rational estimates based on the clearest set of assumptions you can form. The month in which your gross sales equals your calculated break-even is the month in which your business stops being a loss operation and starts moving into a profit. Virtually all new businesses will start out at a loss, simply because it takes awhile to get started, and for new customers to find out where your business is and that you are providing goods and services which will satisfy their wants and needs. It is essential to predict as accurately as possible how long it will take for your start-up operation to reach its break-even point, because the sum of the monthly operating deficits up to that point will help you to determine how much working capital you will require for your business. For an ongoing business, past sales experience is a good guide here as well. Seasonal fluctuations will remain fairly constant from year to year. If your pattern differs from the industry averages, try to determine why. Often this will help you recast your own sales efforts in a more profitable way.

Some important questions to ask about your sales level:

1. How fast will sales grow? Will they decline or stabilize?
2. How rapidly can you develop new customers and will it pay?
3. What is the average sale per customer; can it be increased?
4. What is the frequency of repeat sales; can it be increased?
5. What is the state of the economy in general; in your own industry?
6. Are there cyclical trends in your industry? How can they (and how did they) affect you?
7. What is the nature of your competition? Is it getting stronger, declining, is new competition entering the market?

It is important to note that forecasting is based on coherent review and rational analysis. These allow you to control your business better and manage change more efficiently.

One of the ways to project when you will reach the break-even point is to use a graph (see Figure 4-4). Plot a line on that graph that seems to you to be a reasonable growth curve. The point at which the line crosses the break-even is, again, the point at which you will break even (no profit, no loss). The business shown in Figure 4-4 would break even in the sixth month.

Customer projections

Another way of achieving the same result is by calculating how many new customers can be added per month, how many old customers will be retained, the frequency of repeat sales, and the average dollar sale per customer. Suppose you have a start-up:

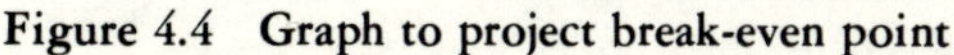
Figure 4.4 Graph to project break-even point

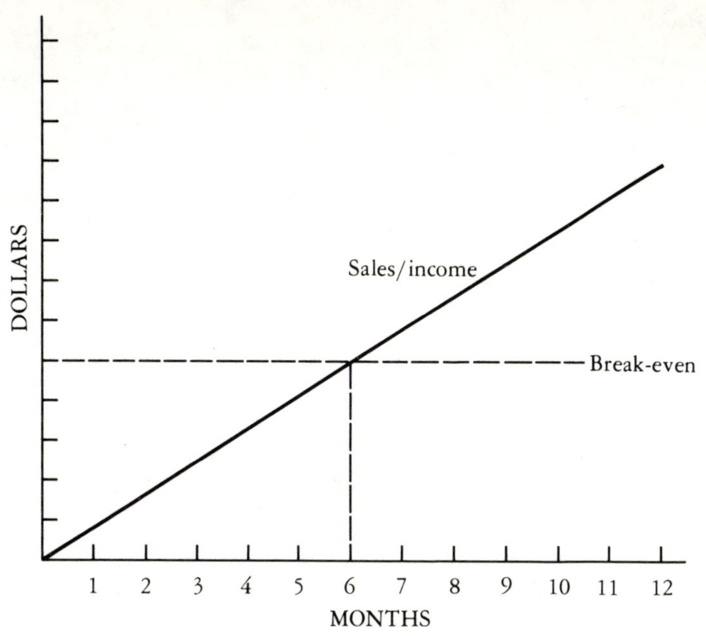

Month	*1*	*2*	*3*	*4*	*5*	*6*
# Customers	10	15	20	30	45	50
New	10	5	5	10	15	5
Old	0	10	15	20	30	45

Assuming that you will never lose a customer, that frequency of repeat sales is one per month, and that the average sale per customer is $75.00, gross sales would grow as follows:

Month								
1	$75	×	10	×	1	=	$ 750
2	$75	×	15	×	1	=	1,125
3	$75	×	20	×	1	=	1,500
4	$75	×	30	×	1	=	2,250
5	$75	×	45	×	1	=	3,375
6	$75	×	50	×	1	=	3,750

Plotting these projections will yield the growth curve shown in Figure 4-5.

Figure 4-5. Growth curve based on customer projections

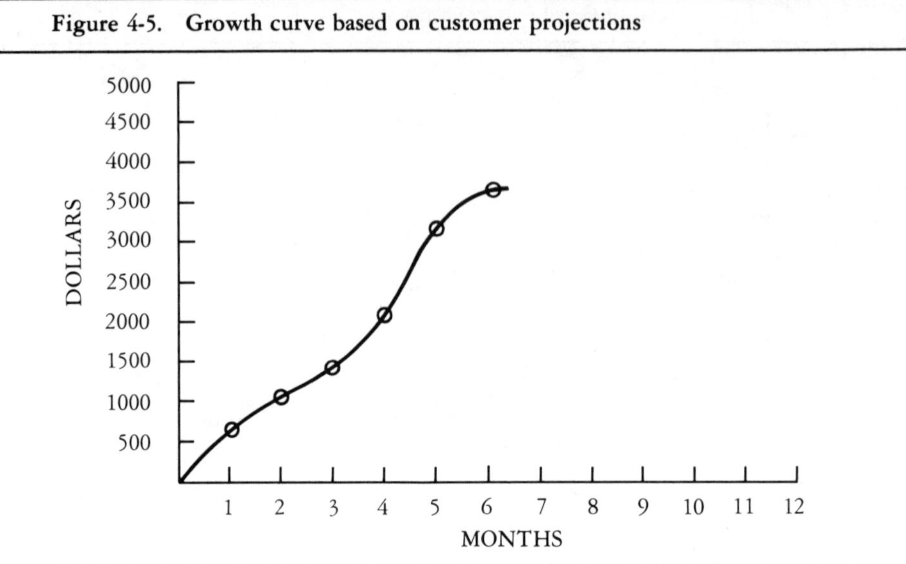

It would be assumed that the rate of sales would begin to flatten as the trend extended into the future, and an indication of the break-even level can be added as well (Figure 4-6). According to the diagram, break-even occurs between the fifth and the sixth month.

You may have noticed that the assumption of never losing a customer is built in; is this reasonable for your business? Probably not, yet many businesses proceed as if that were the case.

Figure 4-6. Growth curve showing break-even point

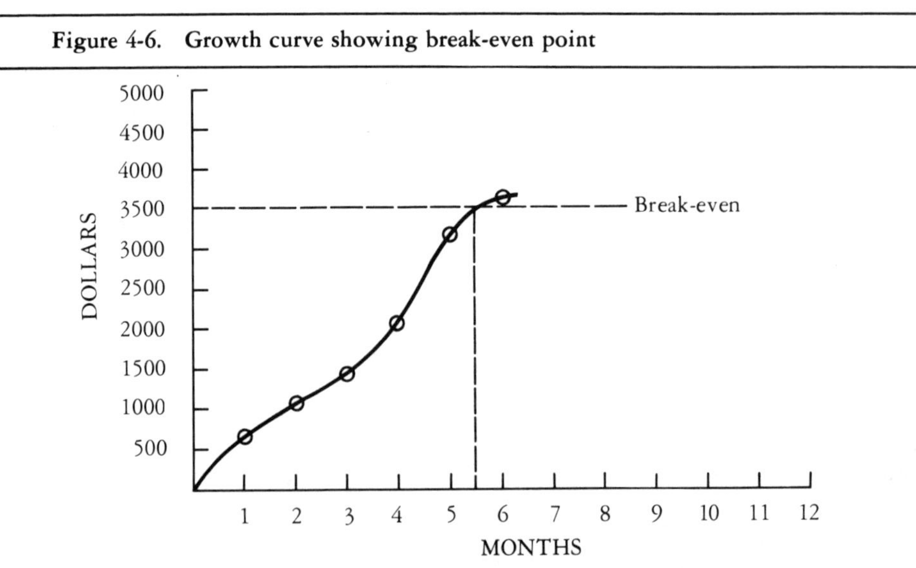

Cyclical variations

Some industries have cycles throughout the year where sales regularly move up and/or down. In the men's wear business, for example, the business cycles peak in the spring and in the fall with the introduction of new seasonal styles (Figure 4-7).

Figure 4-7. Seasonal cycles in the men's wear industry

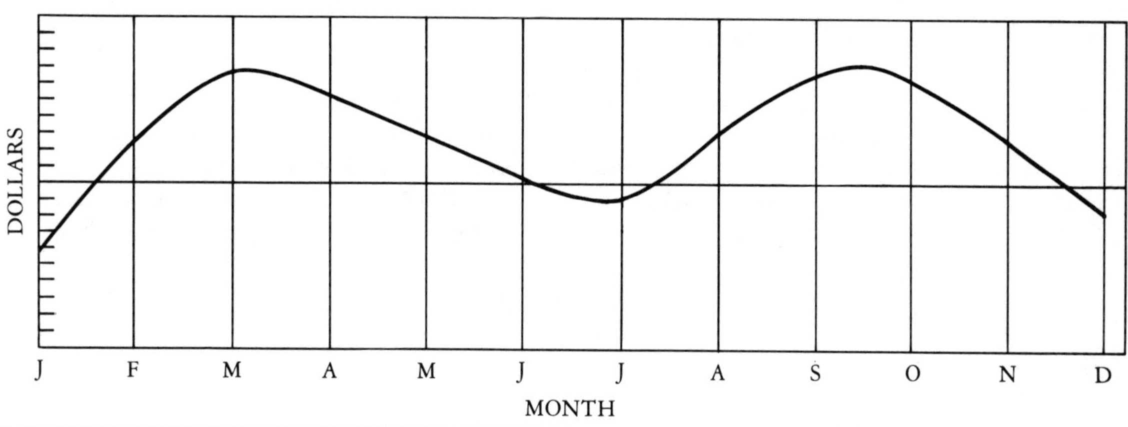

Another example of cyclical variations is the construction industry, which has a seasonal peak in the fall and tapers off during the winter (Figure 4-8).

Figure 4-8. Seasonal cycles in the construction industry

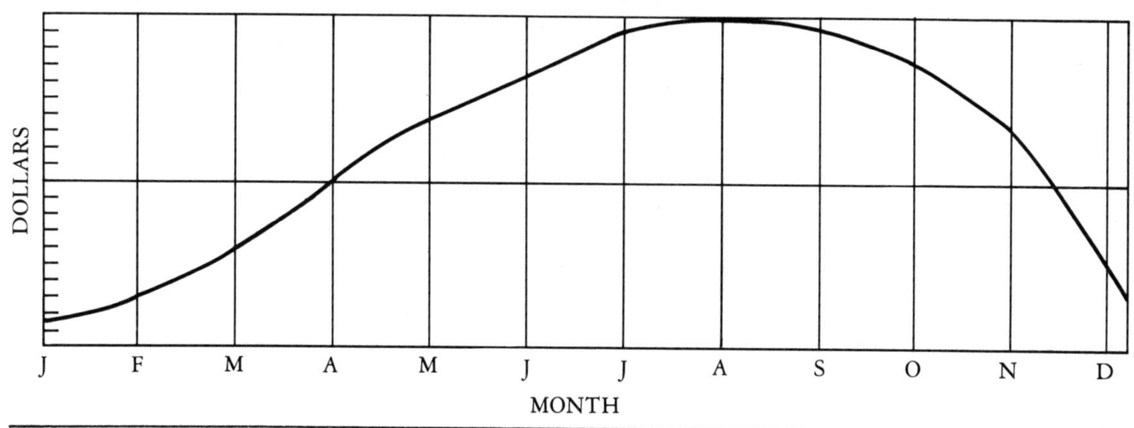

Consider these cycles to determine how your own business will be influenced by seasonal fluctuations for the industry you are in. Your forecast curve may not exactly reflect the industry pattern because you are a start-up, but even this initial growth will probably be influenced by the seasonal variations. The point is that the more you begin developing your understanding of how your business will behave, the more of this type of information you can bring to bear on your analysis, and the more accurate your analysis will be.

If you treat each step of the forecasting process as a new opportunity to check your assumptions, making a systematic attempt to ferret out and reconsider all of the assumptions, you cannot help but improve your business's performance.

Step 5: Consider your downside risk.

A contingency reserve is in your backup working capital. Most businesses lose money when they start up. Expansions usually behave similarly. By definition, these situations will lose money until they reach their break-even level of sales. The amount of this loss can be calculated through your cash-flow analysis and is the amount that you must have available to invest in the business as working capital. If it takes longer to reach the break-even level than you first anticipated, the loss will continue for a longer period of time and you will have to invest more capital to cover that operating deficit. If this occurs, then you

Figure 4-9. Break-even graph showing contingency reserve

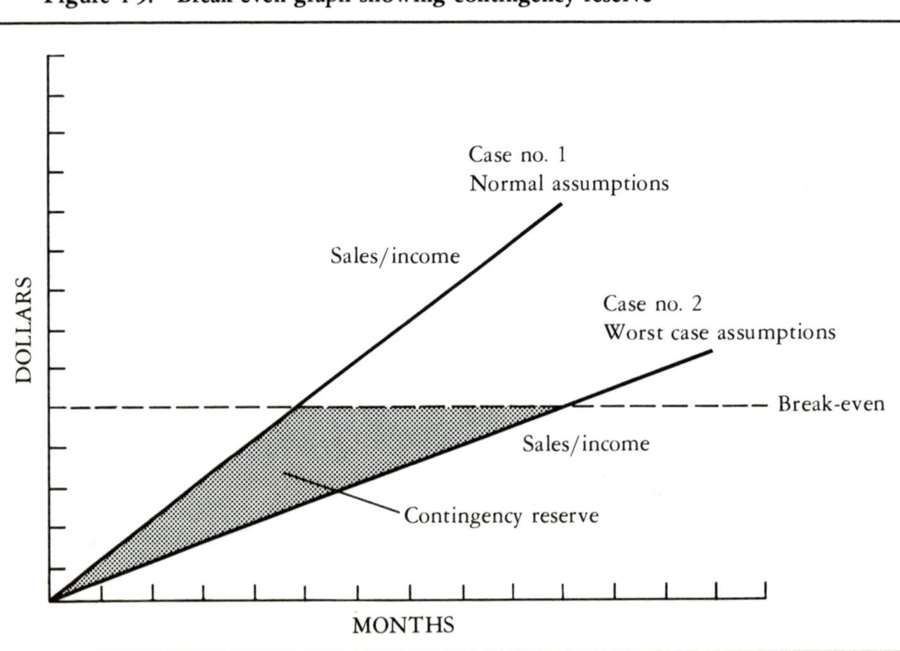

must have this additional working capital available as a cash or contingency reserve. *The contingency reserve is the difference between reasonable and pessimistic assumptions which will show you the necessary cash reserves.* The growth curve that you have plotted in step 4 may seem reasonable for your business operation. However, it is only prudent to consider also what could happen if anything goes wrong, especially if sales are not generated as rapidly as you expect they might be.

To consider your "downside risk," plot a second sales line based on minimal sales expectations (worst-case assumptions) on your break-even graph (Figure 4-4) in addition to the sales line based on reasonable expectations. The result is shown in Figure 4-9. The area between the two sales lines will indicate the amount of contingency reserve that you would be wise to carry.

Step 6: Translate the graphs into income forecasts.

The parts of the process for making income forecasts have now been assembled. In step 1, you identified your fixed and variable expenses. In step 2 through step 5, you experimented with different ways of constructing sales forecasts. Using these understandings, now you will continue these steps so that you can inspect the changes that you expect in your business month by month. This will show you the actual profit or loss which you can expect from your venture. This will be your projected, or pro forma, income statement as shown in Figure 4-10.

Figure 4-10. Pro forma income statement translated from sales forecast

Month	1	2	3	4	5	6	Total (6 mo.)
Sales	750	1125	1500	2250	3375	3750	12750
Less: Variable expenses (40%)	300	450	600	900	1350	1500	5700
Gross profit (60%)	450	675	900	1350	2025	2250	7650
Less: Fixed expenses	2130	2130	2130	2130	2130	2130	12780
Net profit (loss)	(1680)	(1455)	(1230)	(780)	(105)	120	(5130)
Cumulative profit (loss)	(1680)	(3135)	(4365)	(5145)	(5250)	(5130)	

You will notice that the example gives a profit or loss for any given month, and also shows the cumulative profit or loss for the entire operation up to that point. It is very important to be able to think about both of these figures. Just because your business moves past its break-even and begins to show a profit does not mean that you are out of the woods. You must still cover the losses that you have accumulated up to that point; in Figure 4-10, the business shows a loss for the first five months. This is typical for most start-up situations. In fact, it often takes longer than this to show a profit, frequently up to nine months, and, in some businesses, well over a year. . . even more. It simply takes awhile to develop your customer base and to get established. It is also possible that your earlier expenses may be higher than they will be later on. You will need to gain some experience and learn what is necessary and important to the business along with learning the most efficient ways of performing the various activities necessary to run the operation.

Step 7: Translate the income forecasts into a cash flow.

The cash flow is the single most important part of the forecasting process for a new or proposed business, or for any business which is undergoing rapid change. The projected cash flow is the basis of your cash budget. It shows the timing of cash flows and enables you to make sure that you will have adequate cash reserves as well as working capital. For a new venture or for a rapidly growing business, the odds approach certainty that cash will flow out more rapidly than it comes in. This, of course, represents a common way to go broke. The difference between the cash inflows and the cash outflows must come from somewhere. If it is not available in the form of working capital or cash reserves, then you will simply run out of cash and go under, even though you may be selling more and more and even though these sales may be proceeding on a profitable basis.

Cash-flow forecasting enables you to predict both the size and timing of this kind of temporary operating deficit. By adding to this figure a cushion for unexpected emergencies (Step 5), you can calculate how much cash reserve you will need to remain solvent.

For the purposes of an example, assume that all of your sales are on credit and that everyone pays his bill within the thirty-day credit terms which you have made available. (This, of course, often does not hold true. Generally, the repayment will take longer.) The impact of these credit sales can be inspected through the cash flow analysis. This is illustrated in Figure 4-11.

Figure 4-11. Pro forma cash flow

Month	1	2	3	4	5	6	Total
Cash receipts		750	1125	1500	2250	3375	9000
Less: Cash disbursements							
Variable expenses	300	450	600	900	1350	1500	5100
Fixed expense	2130	2130	2130	2130	2130	2130	12780
Total cash disbursements	2430	2580	2730	3030	3480	3630	17880
Net cash flow	(2430)	(1830)	(1605)	(1530)	(1230)	(255)	(8880)
Cumulative cash flow	(2430)	(4260)	(5865)	(7395)	(8625)	(8880)	

In the XYZ Company, Inc., pro forma income statement (Figure 4-10), the business shows a profit in the sixth month even though the cumulative is not covered within the forecast period. However, according to the cash flow analysis shown in Figure 4-11, the business does not reach its cash break-even at all and so is not able to cover its cumulative negative cash flows during the forecast period. This illustrates a critical aspect of cash planning that many businesses simply ignore. Profitability does not necessarily equal liquidity. Consequently, businesses which are making profits may go out of business because they run out of cash. Here is the important distinction between profitability and liquidity. The pro forma income statement will illustrate the profitability of the venture; the pro forma cash flow analysis will indicate the liquidity of the venture. For most new or rapidly changing business situations, liquidity will be a far more pressing concern than profitability. Liquidity problems can be anticipated. If they are anticipated, you can decide in advance what you are going to do about them.

Summary

Forecasting is based on carefully reasoned assumptions quantified in a systematic way to make your projections for what will happen in the future as accurate as possible. Forecasting has been described as a seven-step process which is based on a methodical application and assessment of available information.

By taking a systematic approach to forecasting, you will gain a deeper knowledge and understanding of your business. The final product of your forecasting effort becomes your projected cash flow, the basis of the cash budget, which, in turn, is a primary tool for controlling your business.

The purpose of the forecasting process is twofold: It affords an excellent opportunity to review the past, and it provides the best guide to the future that your business can have. Anticipating problems and avoiding them, rather than waiting until they arrive and then trying to deal with them on a reactive basis, is the essence of good business planning, and good business planning is one of the keys to business success.

5. CASH FLOW

WHAT IS CASH FLOW?

In its simplest form, *cash flow refers to the flows of cash, literally, into and out of the business.* The sources of cash (inflow) are limited to—

new investment
new debt
sale of fixed assets
operating profits

There really are no other sources that can be appealed to when times are hard. Inspecting this list will show that, clearly, each of these sources has important limitations on it as well. The only source that can be depended on in an ongoing fashion is operating profits, and that is what makes profit planning such an important activity for any business. It is only by profitable operation and only when that profitable operation is accompanied by a positive cash flow that the business can grow.

On the other hand, the cash outflows are as varied and idiosyncratic as businesses and business owners. The more obvious outflows are found on the income statement as expenses, except for such noncash items as depreciation. By definition, noncash items are not part of your cash flow. One item to be added to other expenses is the principal portion of loan payments which, while it is not an expense item, is still a use of cash. The most useful way to conceptualize this process is to think of actual cash, dollar bills, flowing in and out of the business, and then to identify their sources and identify their uses. That is *cash flow analysis.* Cash flow analysis is described here as an eight-step process which will help you understand your own business better. For many users, this provides a slightly different view than they have had of their business before. In addition to improving profits, cash flow analysis is particularly useful in helping to cope with seasonal fluctuations and to avoid money crunches caused by rapid growth. The underlying objective of the process is to make your business planning and operation more profitable.

WHY CASH FLOW?

Why is cash flow so important? If the cash inflows exceed the cash outflows, your business can continue operations. If the cash outflows exceed the inflows, your business runs out of cash and grinds to a halt. Even if the imbalance lasts only a short time, it can spell disaster.

Cash management, controlling the cash flow, is vital to businesses of all sizes. Small businesses are especially vulnerable to cash flow problems since they tend to operate with inadequate cash reserves or none at all, and, worse, to miss the implications of a negative cash flow until it's too late.

Timing and cash flow are inseparable (see Figure 5-1). Your suppliers probably expect payments even before your customers pay you. As a result, you are very likely to have

Figure 5-1. The cash flow cycle

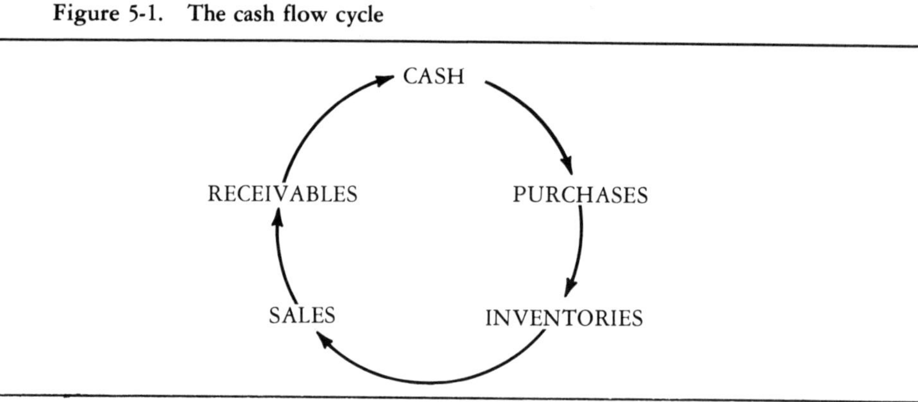

a negative cash flow when your business grows dramatically. Periods of change are always reflected in an altered cash flow. If sales fall off, the cash flow slows down; if sales increase, the cash flow may possibly stop completely or even become negative. Think of the impact of credit sales on your cash flow, for example. Seasonal fluctuations in your business may pose cash flow problems where you would need to provide for a build-up in front of a seasonal period of demand, requiring investments in inventories or other expenses before you are able to reap the benefit of sales.

Whatever the cause, the underlying message is simple: Run out of cash and you are in trouble. Even if you can promote more money, sooner or later you must match the timing of cash inflows and outflows if you are to remain in operation.

How do you get your cash flow under control? It's not easy. Some businesses never achieve cash flow control. These businesses are always in trouble, chronically overdrawn, and slow in paying bills, and they will eventually fold. They fold, though, only after their owner/managers have spent a great deal of their time worrying and probably spending all of their personal assets trying to cover the operating deficits. This kind of hassle need not be an integral part of business management. Instead, plan and schedule so that cash flow for your business is positive.

If you suffer from one or more of the following, you have a cash flow problem:

1. decreased liquidity: running out of working capital
2. overtrading: turning inventories over more than trade average
3. excessive reliance on short-term debt
4. dropped discounts: over term payables
5. slow collections: elderly receivables

HOW TO MANAGE CASH: THE EIGHT STEPS

The process of cash flow management does not need to be mysterious or complex. Cash flow management is timing inflows and outflows. Control will naturally follow from cash flow planning. The following eight-step process has been designed to show the sequence of activities and how they can be applied in any business situation in order to bring about this desired required control.

Eight steps of cash flow management

1. List cash inflows (sources).
2. List cash outflows (uses).
3. Identify when (by date) cash flows in or out.
4. Examine timing: cash inflows minus cash outflows.
5. Identify the major consequences of cash as it currently flows.
6. Show constraints: inflows or outflows which cannot be changed.
7. Identify inflows and outflows which can be changed or rescheduled.
8. Establish a plan for positive cash flow.

These eight steps take time and thought. Without this investment of your own energy, they will not work. It is important to take the time to experiment with combinations of different alternatives. The end result of this process, a controlled cash flow, will more than repay the time and effort you give to it. In fact, it may save the life of your business and your own future as well.

Step 1: List cash inflows (sources).

While new investment and new debt are sources of cash, they are infrequent and limited. They cannot be relied on as permanent or repeat sources. The same is true of the sale of fixed assets. They can only be sold once. These three sources are not to be ignored, but they are secondary to operating profits.

The process of financing, generally meaning the use of bank or other sources of credit, is a major management technique and is generally recognized as being important in the structuring of almost any business. For any of these different types of bank credit, and for trade credit, the most important type of small business credit for many, the main interest of these potential sources of funds in your business is how you will be able to repay your debts. The answer to that comes out of your cash flow.

Consequently, it is important to focus on operations as your main source of cash. Operating profit, unlike new investment or debt or sale of fixed assets, is ongoing. As such, it is also harder to keep track of. Since it is ongoing, it must be constantly monitored, reviewed, and controlled.

As a rule-of-thumb, money flows into profitable businesses and away from unprofitable ones. Although a stable operation which makes a profit will usually not have any cash flow problems, any business which grows dramatically will. Growth, unless carefully financed, can put a profitable business into bankruptcy even as the income statement shows a growing profit. This represents a real tragedy. A business which is growing and making profits can suffer liquidity problems (the cash runs out), fail to meet its obligations, and then be forced to shut down.

Why? Suppose you offer forty-five-day terms to your customers (or they take forty-five—it works out the same way), while you must pay your suppliers on the terms they offer, thirty days or even cash (C.O.D). As sales grow, so will your receivables. Meanwhile, you continue your own payables on a current basis, and the gap between payables and receivables gets wider and wider in negative cash flow. Soon you will run out of cash.

It is possible to avoid this problem, and that is what cash flow management is all about. Timing and operations go together. It may be very possible, as you analyze your operations, that you will discover that a small customer who pays promptly is more profitable to you than a large customer who pays slowly.

Cash flow problems are frequently caused by collection problems. If you have many chronic slow-payers (a condition endemic to some industries), either step up your collection efforts, find some other way of speeding up that cash flow (perhaps through the use of discounts), or consider the possibilities of factoring or some other form of accounts receivable financing.

In any case, if you have one or more large slow-paying customers, analyze the account. It may be costing you cash by tying up cash that you can't afford to have tied up. Even though it may seem crazy, you may have to stop doing business with a customer like this. The more he purchases, the less you can afford to handle his orders.

Another problem that begins to sneak up on many businesses is that the period in which your customers pay their bills begins to get longer and longer. This problem can be identified in its development stages through an ongoing process of *aging the receivables.* This will help you spot the slow-paying and the super-slow-paying customers. Aging receivables is done by listing your accounts receivables in categories according to when they were originally invoiced, 30, 60, 90, 120, and more days. If you are not aware of slow-paying customers, it's difficult to improve your collection efforts. Incidentally, successful accounts-receivable collection efforts are often only a phone call or two away, although sometimes letters of a more formal nature or a small-claims court appearance may be needed.

Another area of operations to examine closely is *inventory.* It is often wise to take advantage of special bulk rate offers. At the same time, it is important to recognize that you may end up buying problems. A bloated inventory will slow anyone's cash flow down needlessly. There is a companion problem with inventory management which is the reverse of the first. This problem comes about by trying to make a slim inventory and too little capital work overtime. This is *overtrading,* and its usual result is disaster. Overtrading is likely to result in stockouts which will discourage and perhaps lose customers, and an inability to take advantage of volume discounts for purchases or shipping. As a consequence of this overtrading problem, if just one customer fails to pay on time, the entire business blows apart.

In summary, list your cash inflows, either by product or by customer or both. This will help you to identify trouble spots which snag your cash flow and, in combination with an aging of your receivables, will begin to focus your attention on the timing of your cash flow.

Step 2: List cash outflows (uses).

The places to start examining your cash outflows are your cash journal and your checkbook. If you don't have either of these, you shouldn't be in business. Both, and, simply enough, the checkbook particularly, are the heart of any cash control system.

Cash control failures are relatively rare, although they do impact your cash flow. More frequently, proper business practices which include cash control are followed, but the small business still runs out of money.

The important activity for this step on the process is to determine where the cash is going. This is a serious exercise. Bankers, accountants, and others who get involved in the problem side of small-business cash flow problems all agree that departing from the budget "just this once" is a leading killer of small businesses because bending the budget rapidly becomes a habit.

There are many variations of this theme: petty cash accounts that amount to 50 percent of gross sales, salary increases which bear no relationship to productivity and profits, a new Oriental carpet for the office, even long trips to buy lunches in New York City (because big businessmen lunch in New York?)—the list is endless.

Put it all down. Track down as many of the expenses as possible and begin to ask, "Is this expense necessary? Can we get along without it? Postpone it? Is the timing okay? Would it make more sense to pay for it earlier or later? Can it be done less expensively?"

The answers here may save you some money immediately. We all tend to fall into habits. Habits can help us to be efficient, but some habits are costly. Paying bills as they come in is one habit that many small businesses fall into. Prompt payment is fine, but, if your customers are paying on a forty-five-day basis while you pay on a five-day basis, your cash flow is being pinched unnecessarily.

Timing is the essence of this matter. Ideally, inflows are slightly faster than outflows; however, over a period of time, they must at least balance.

If you cannot determine where your cash is going, you need better and more timely information. Your accounting system should contain the answers here. If you don't have an accounting system you can't determine what is happening. This is the time to see your friendly accountant and get him to help you structure a system that will provide you with the information that you require.

For many smaller businesses, a checkbook can provide an adequate daily record of cash disbursements. So-called "one-write" systems are checkbooks which have a carbon block on the back of each check or which use mark-sensitive paper to automatically record each transaction in your journal. This forces you to identify as you write the check the account that the expenditure should be charged to, rather than try to remember what happened at the end of the month. A one-write system may be satisfactory for many businesses but inadequate for others. Your accountant should help you design an accounting system that serves your needs for information about your business. If your accountant isn't cooperative, doesn't help you produce information in a timely manner, or doesn't answer your questions, get another accountant. These professionals work for you and must be responsive to your needs. You have responsibilities as well. It's your business, and, if you don't cooperate with them, they can't do their jobs. If you can't afford this type of help, you shouldn't be in business. These expenses are just as relevant and just as critical as rent or any of the other more obvious expenditures, and yet, many small businesses look at them as unnecessary and avoid them generally at a serious cost to their own ability to manage their own business.

Step 3: Identify when (by date) cash flows in or out.

The most useful tool for this step of the process is a calendar. Get one large enough to make notations in each date block and begin to list according to their timing the major cash inflows and outflows you have discovered in the first two steps. To be most useful, one full business cycle should be displayed. For most businesses, especially those with any sort of cyclical variation, a year will be a useful period of time to be examined, although monthly or perhaps even weekly periods may be relevant units of time for inspection.

A handy technique here is to begin by listing those fixed outflows which have fixed dates: paydays, tax deposits, bank debt repayments, insurance payments, and perhaps other obligations. Begin listing these dates as you think of them. Keep listing over a period of time, because your list will not be complete the first few times you try this. You simply won't think of everything. It is sometimes suggested that this be done in a rough fashion with 3 × 5 cards. This allows you to begin shuffling the cards, quite literally, as you begin examianing the timing of these cash outflows, and perhaps begin to realize that some of the fixed payment dates are more flexible than they may first appear.

Once the payment dates, or cash outflow dates, are known you can start listing cash inflows. This will result in a conservative cash flow if you allow for your receivable experience and your seasonal or periodic sales fluctuations. Your aim must be to balance inflows and outflows to suit the peculiarities of your own business. If you can achieve this, then you will be able to grow with minimum interference from creditors and maximum ability to take advantage of opportunities that may occur in your own business situation.

Step 4: Examine timing: Cash inflows minus cash outflows.

A positive cash flow is one in which inflows are ahead of outflows (see Figure 5-1). This must be true not just as an average over the year, but consistently throughout the normal business cycle. The reality is that any negative cash flow for any operating period must be funded from somewhere. That funding may come from a ninety-day note or from the normal operating cash balances, but it must be available. If it is not available, then the business has a problem.

This is not to say that an occasional negative cash flow will spell trouble. There are times when it makes more sense to adopt a negative cash flow temporarily (in a growth spurt, for example) than always to structure operations conservatively so that these negative cash balances will never appear. However, you must maintain a positive cash flow more often than not, and again, be prepared to subsidize those deficit periods or negative cash flows when they do occur.

Most businesses have a rhythm. Farmers need time to grow their product, then wait for payment, then receive a sum of money which is used to pay off old debt, make necessary improvements and purchases, and perhaps even to relax with. At the time they have no cash inflows, they have substantial outflows, ongoing expenses which cannot be shifted but which must be paid as and when they become due, such as seed, fertilizer, and, particularly, labor. As a consequence, many farmers have a chronic cash flow problem.

In many states, contractors are in a similar situation. They must register their heavy equipment in March, at the commencement of their earning period, which is at the end of a long nonearning spell.

Some of these payment clusters are unavoidable; some may even be desirable, but, in the long run, it is the balance, the timing, which is critical.

Consider the patterns of the two companies shown in Figure 5-2. Company A's sales are level or increasing slowly, making a modest profit, and Company B's sales are zooming with rapidly growing profits but an increasing liquidity problem. The level Company A will plod along growing slowly; the rapidly growing Company B will find money trickling in and flooding out. Payables tend to fall due faster than receivables can be collected. It is possible through this process to be so successful that you go broke. The business becomes illiquid, and you run out of cash.

Your historical purchasing and sales rhythms must be understood, thought through, and compared with your industry patterns. If you are seriously out of phase with your industry, then you had best be doubly careful because those patterns are powerful and are not easily changed. Average patterns you should be familiar with and compare your

Figure 5-2. A comparison of patterns of cash flow timing

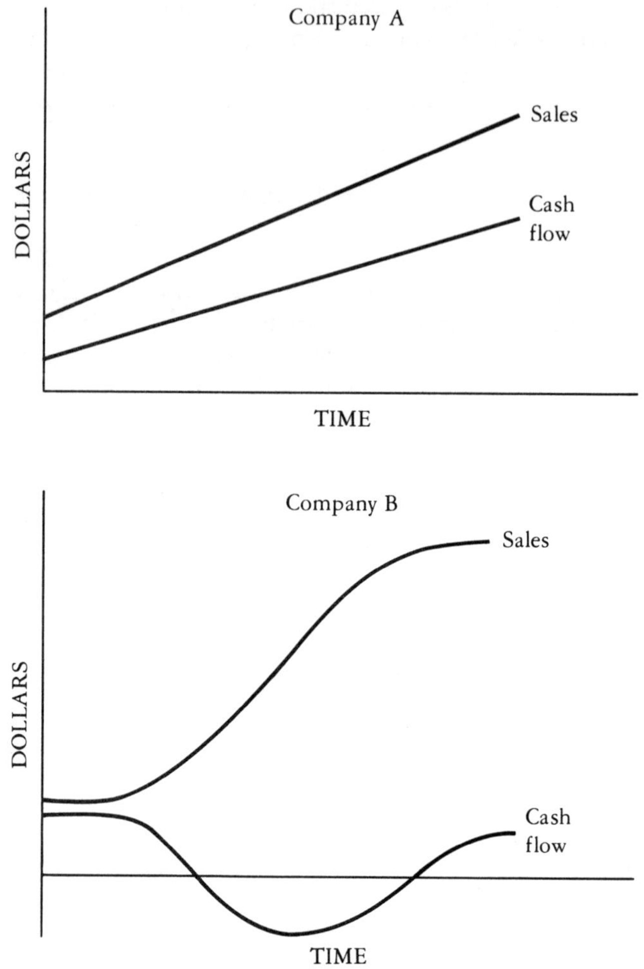

business to are listed in such sources as the *ACA Barometer of Small Business* and *RMA Annual Statement Studies* (see Appendix D).

One important result of this step is that you will be able to determine how fast you can afford to grow. This may seem paradoxical since many businesses see their major problem in trying to determine how they can grow faster, but businesses with a substantial amount of market demand may instead have to consider ways of repressing this growth. Assuming a positive cash flow (cash inflows exceeding cash outflows), and assuming that growth uses cash, you can then grow at the rate that the inflows exceed the outflows. If you attempt to grow at a rate faster than this, you will simply run out of cash. Growth planning as well as survival planning needs to be a carefully structured process.

Step 5: Identify the major consequences of cash as it currently flows.

Performing this step does not so much require numerical calculations as it requires honesty about your actual operations. For many, this may become an unpleasant, surprising, or discouraging confrontation with reality.

The greatest problems small businesses have with cash flows stem from the human tendency to believe that because you try to pay your bills on time so does everyone else. That is admirable, but it is dangerous as well. It is more reasonable to expect that your customers will pay slowly. They have their own problems and other reasons for doing so. General advice here is to plan on payments being slower than you reasonably expect.

Everyone in business (almost) knows that one way to improve cash flow is to slow down the outflow while speeding up the inflow, particularly in a tightening economy. The result is that payments are slow all the way around. You can plan on it.

Subcontractors find this a way of life, especially those who subcontract to government contractors. It is a cost of doing business which can be fatal unless it is anticipated. In fact, it is possible to turn this type of situation around to your own advantage. For example, one small wholesaler who sold housing products to large contractors more than doubled his profit by taking note of this fact. He arranged both trade and bank credit around an anticipated eighteen-month payment cycle (Figure 5-3). As the major contractors were

Figure 5-3. An eighteen-month cash flow cycle

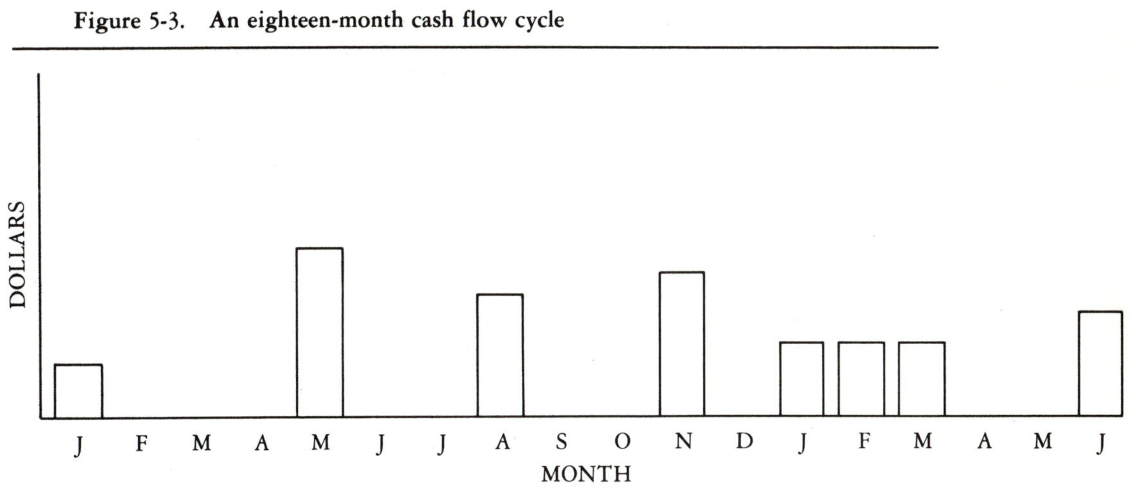

on twelve-month contracts, this worked out well. They were paid in stages over fifteen months, and his receivables came in a month or so later than theirs. His credit improved because he paid off his obligations on a timely basis, and he made more money by borrowing wisely.

Planning your cash flow is profitable. By looking at the timing of cash inflows and outflows, you will find ways to improve your profits by both cutting costs and by increasing your opportunities. However, you cannot plan unless you are aware of your industry patterns. Another major problem, particularly for small retailers, is cuff credit, the credit businesses extend to their customers. Businesses frequently feel obliged to extend credit when they actually cannot afford to tie up their working capital in this manner, and may in fact not need to provide this cuff service at all. Credit decisions are best made by professionals, and most small businesses do not have such professionals on their staff. Ask your banker about bank credit-card arrangements. Perhaps by taking the standard discount (around 3 to 3½ percent) you will speed up your cash flow and gain enough new customers to more than offset the perceived extra servicing costs of maintaining a bank-card program, and you will also avoid the collection problems and other attendant carrying costs.

It is important to note also that the costs of participating in these bank credit-card plans are often negotiable, just as are the interest rates of loans. Many small businesses do not realize this and quietly and happily accept whatever rate their banker quotes to them. It makes good sense to do some comparison shopping for these credit purchases, just as you would do for any other item you must buy for your business. After all, why should you pay more than you have to?

Credit patterns take different forms. For example, consumer credit payments tend to lag around Christmas and again around the summer vacation months, pick up in the spring as tax refunds come out, and pick up again in the fall. It is almost impossible for a small retailer to handle that kind of seasonal shift unless he is fully aware of it, and all too often it is impossible for him to handle it even if he is. These difficulties reinforce the earlier advice: leave the credit business to those who make it their business.

Step 6: Show constraints: inflows or outflows which cannot be changed.

Not every payment can be rescheduled (see step 7 for further discussion), and not every collection effort pays off. Your cash flow planning must respect these fixed constraints.

By identifying the most likely sticky places in the cash flow both by analyzing the past and by planning the future, you can prevent the real disasters of cash flow blockage. You won't have a lot of luck altering tax dates, and tinkering whimsically with payday is not legal. Insurance payments follow a rigid schedule. If you have agreed to this schedule and then miss a payment, your insurance may be cancelled.

Identify the apparently inflexible outflows. Some will be necessary; some may not be. List them; plan around them. If they are really necessary and inflexible, then you have no choice.

With cash inflows, the matter is different. While it is not always possible to speed up cash inflows, it is possible to identify those customers who create snags and then deal with them on a one-by-one basis. Over a period of time, this can significantly help your cash flow, but it must be done consistently and selectively. Every smaller business with any kind of credit activity undoubtedly has customers that it cannot afford to maintain. Even if these customers eventually pay up, sales and growth opportunities may well be lost while they have tied up working capital and slowed down the cash flows.

A horrible example of this was a service-station owner who allowed his customers to run up substantial cuff-credit accounts and then watched these customers, embarrassed at their inability to pay off the account, go to his competitors and pay cash.

Cash flow management is timing inflows and outflows. A positive cash flow is essential. A negative cash flow over a period of time is fatal.

Step 7: Identify inflows and outflows which can be changed or rescheduled.

At this stage, your major, fixed cash-flow points have been listed, your timing examined, your rhythms explored, and the business habits that affect cash flow carefully scrutinized. Now try to determine if any of these factors can be changed. It is natural to think that, because something has always been done on a certain schedule in the past, that is how it must always be. This is not necessarily true. There is much to be said for not paying bills on the first and the fifteenth. A good example of this is the situation of a car dealer who found himself caught in a cash squeeze caused by growth and needed an additional $30,000 in working capital. His business was sound and could afford the debt. However, an outside consultant determined through an analysis of the business that the owner really didn't need the loan. He paid his bills as they were received, a noble but unnecessary habit; the custom in the trade was "net 30." It was also noted that his purchases were averaging $30,000 per month. The consultant's advice to this person was, "Don't pay your bills for one month." He followed this advice, got his needed $30,000 in working capital, and saved his borrowing capacity for some other need. He also saved himself over $3,000 a year in annual interest charges that the new debt would have incurred. This is not to suggest that businesses stop paying their bills, but it does illustrate that, if you analyze your own bill-paying activities, you may discover that you can take advantage of the same kind of opportunity. This is one of the positive consequences of this cash management/cash planning activity.

There is merit in talking with your creditors and working out a payment schedule which fits your needs, not theirs. A surprising number of larger companies and banks are happy to work out such arrangements. If they can help their smaller-business customers prosper and grow, they will prosper too.

Suppose your analysis has shown that in June and November you have extra cash, while in March you are chronically short. Balloon payments (Figure 5-4) are helpful in this kind of situation. Another useful technique is to preplan nonpayment months. Your larger creditors are interested in their own cash flow, and what they need to know most is when they will be paid. They have experts studying this problem. You can take advantage of their skills only if you discuss your situation with them. If that March payment is going to be uncomfortably tight, let them know well in advance, replan your payment schedule, and you will both be better off for it. You will also find that your relationship with these supplier creditors improves dramatically.

There are ways that you can change your customers' paying habits to be more in your favor as well. Ask your banker for credit help; he should know or be able to tell you

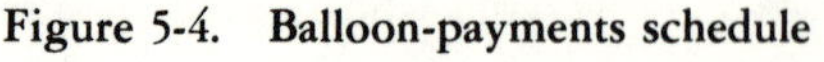

Figure 5-4. Balloon-payments schedule

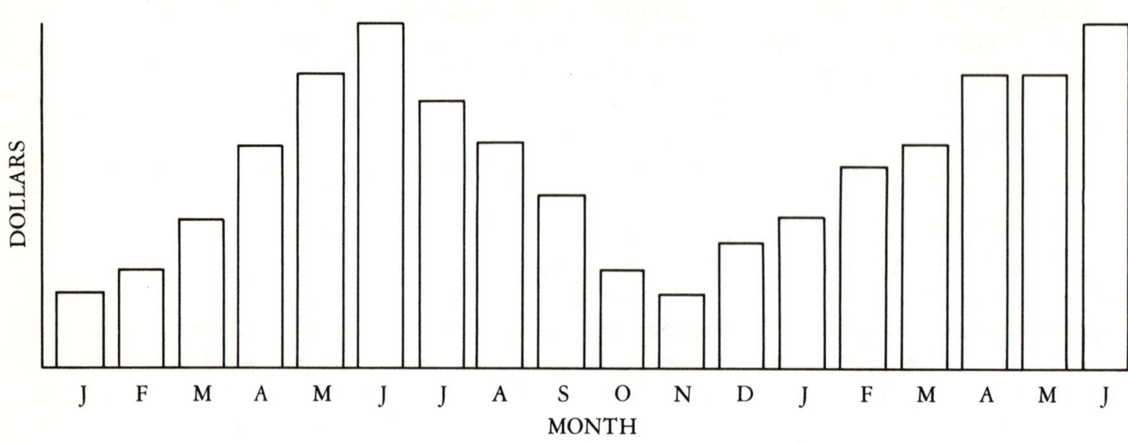

who can help with decisions such as offering discounts, partial payment plans, credit cards, billing and collection arrangements, selling receivables to a factor, finance company, or other financing house, or with any of the other myriad ways to speed up cash inflows and restore a cash flow balance. Some of these techniques are expensive, and some not appropriate or even possible for certain types of business. They are not to be undertaken lightly or adopted wholesale as a panacea. They are to be studied carefully and utilized when and if appropriate.

Another important source of advice and assistance may be your own trade association. The odds are good that if you have a problem with customers who pay slowly, so do your colleagues. Trade organizations represent a resource which you can and should utilize.

The key is timing. Slow down the outflow, speed up the inflow, and make sure that the process is not a one-time effort. It must be monitored constantly, and small, regular, relatively insignificant corrective activities are far more productive than massive, one-time corrective actions. It is much easier to keep your customers from becoming delinquent than to try to get them to pay once they have become old and troubled accounts.

Step 8: Establish a plan for positive cash flow.

This final step involves going back to your large calendar and repeating step 3 with more detail.

First: Indicate the cash flow items which cannot be changed to other dates.

Second: List your anticipated cash inflows allowing a margin for safety. If your credit terms provide thirty days for your accounts receivable, plan on a forty-five-day average for safety. Check your historical experience to make sure that this is realistic.

Figure 5-5. Form for cash flow budget

Cash Flow
Budget Deviation Analysis
Period Ending: ____________

MONTH	1		2		3		4		5		6		7		8		9		10		11		12		Total	
	Bud	Act	Bud	Act	Bud	Act	Bud	Act	Bud	Act	Bud	Act	Bud	Act	Bud	Act	Bud	Act	Bud	Act	Bud	Act	Bud	Act	Bud	Act
Cash receipts																										
Sales — cash																										
Accounts receivable																										
Loan receipts																										
New investments																										
Sale of assets																										
Other																										
Total cash receipts																										
Cash disbursements																										
Material/inventories																										
Direct labor																										
Admin. salaries																										
Office salaries																										
Office expense																										
Advertising																										
Trade shows																										
Travel																										
Delivery expense																										
Rent																										
Telephone																										
Electric																										
Heat																										
Equipment repair																										
Facility maintenance																										
Insurance																										
Admin. and legal																										
Taxes and licenses																										
Interest, loans																										
Principal, loans																										
Other interest																										
Other disbursements																										
Miscellaneous																										
Total cash disbursements																										
Net cash flow																										
Cumulative cash flow																										

Third: Allocate payment dates to suit the needs of your particular business. It is generally easy for you to determine when you will be able to repay or meet your obligations. However, once you have agreed to a specific schedule or routine, then make sure that you will be able to honor it. Do not forget to take full advantage of trade credit. For most businesses, it is an excellent source of free working capital, and, for many, one that is not utilized to its fullest extent.

Fourth: Identify the periods of negative cash flow, and determine the actual amounts of the deficiencies. If you have shortfalls or gaps in your schedule where cash outflows will exceed cash inflows, it probably means you have done a realistic job in examining your business operation. You can now plan on how they will be subsidized when they do occur.

Once you have followed the eight steps of cash flow management, you will have the substance and information that you require for establishing your cash flow budget. Forecast on a monthly basis, the cash flow budget becomes one of your most powerful management control tools. Figure 5-5 shows the form generally used to set up such a cash flow budget, and how actual performance can be quickly and easily compared against the budget on a regular basis, especially to point up developing problems, so that you can correct them before they become disasters. The whole secret, of course, is to manage your business and not to let it manage you.

6. FINANCING

WHAT IS FINANCING?

Basically, funds for financing your business operation come in some variation of two forms: (1) *capital,* funds which are permanently invested in the business, and (2) *debt,* funds which are borrowed, rented or leased for business purposes. The purpose in this section is to explain these various types of financing which are needed for different purposes by most small businesses. Certain sources of funds are traditionally used for each different purpose. Different types of funds come from different sources. You must know how much you need of each type before you can start looking for places to get it. There is some specialized terminology as well which you must be familiar with before you can talk intelligently with the suppliers of funds. Definitions of some of the more common terms you may encounter are included here as well.

Bankers customarily divide their lending into three categories. Though there are always exceptions, the categories are fairly uniform:

1. Short-term financing: usually through notes to be paid within one year or less, and paid in one sum
2. Intermediate-term financing: for one to five years, usually repaid on a monthly basis
3. Long-term financing: five or more years, such as real-estate financing, where repayment is made on a schedule over a period of many years

These loans may be secured or unsecured. A *secured loan* is a loan which is backed up by collateral (liens against your property, savings account, investments, perhaps co-signed by someone with more assets or better credit) which, in case you default on your loan, will be applied to the money you still owe. No bank wants to become a secondhand dealer, however, so the usual reason for taking liens against your property is to tie you to the deal, to make it hard for you to give up by upping the stakes. This often proves an unnecessary added worry for a small struggling business, but some bankers like it. An *unsecured loan* is a loan not backed up by collateral. These are almost always for short terms and available only to persons who have proven themselves credit-worthy. The loan is backed up by the bank's faith in your credit and capability of repaying their loan.

It is useful to remember that bankers are in the business of investing money which does not belong to them, money which they must not subject to very much risk. Bankers do not, and should not, gamble with their depositor's money, and you as a borrower must recognize this. When a bank lends you money, it is because it sees your business as one which repays the loan. The banker is not under any obligation to lend money to a business which he perceives to be high risk. This attitude is a frequent source of anger to small businesses. To help your banker decide in your favor, lower the risk: try to make sure that your debt/worth ratio stays low, make sure of enough working capital to cover current liabilities, and match the financing to your need. How? By noting that a loan should be repaid—from the banker's viewpoint—as soon as possible.

Long-term debt is for long-term needs: fixed assets which will be used and paid for over a long period; to pay off this kind of debt too fast is a mistake unless you are extremely well capitalized, in which case ask the banker and your accountant if it is wise. They will tell you.

Short-term debt is for short-term needs: seasonal inventory loans, for one example, and short-run production loans for another. These are paid from the returns on a specific transaction or series of transactions taking place in a short period of time. If these are financed over a long period of time, the result is almost always deepening debt and erosion of the business assets. Even though your cash flow will look fine if you spread the cost over a longer period, you are violating a cardinal rule of borrowing: paying for a benefit after it has been exhausted. Incidentally, one reason bankers are hesitant to bail small businesses out of a pressing trade debt is that that debt remaining unpaid is the clearest evidence possible that the business is mismanaged. Paying for a dead horse is bad business. The *line of credit,* either revolving or non-revolving, is a short-term tool which works like a credit card: you arrange before the need arises to have so much credit to draw against; then you pay it off after a fixed period of time, or turn it over and renew it. The main thing to avoid is getting caught paying for last year's short-term borrowing the next year. This is bad enough when you do it as an individual customer, but it is worse for a small business.

Intermediate-term debt is for those needs which stretch from one to three to five years: most common here are loans for equipment of moderate durability and for working capital loans for businesses undergoing rapid growth. By converting that debt to earnings, and then retaining the earnings, or a portion of them as capital, it is possible to use the bank's money. However, most small businesses should not plan on this, as it requires a farsighted banker indeed, as well as profits large enough to handle a high interest-cost.

A better understanding of types and sources of financing will help you to avoid the four most common abuses of business funds:

1. Undercapitalization
2. Excess debt
3. Insufficient use of credit
4. Friday-night financing

This list is by no means exhaustive. Ever since the invention of money, new ways to fritter away the resources of any business manage to turn up regularly. The most prevalent is lack of control which is apt to be a nickel-and-dime erosion. Abuse of financing is somewhat different. One difference is that it proceeds on a more dramatic scale. Another is that while controls may be imposed at some later date and the bleeding away of money slowed and stopped, the damage from major financial error is much more critical and lasting. Small businesses are almost always undercapitalized or at best slimly capitalized and so are much more susceptible to the negative impact of a substantial mistake than larger organizations which have the financial resources to absorb more than one major error.

WHY FINANCING?

Financing a business is simple enough in concept. You must have adequate funds to enable your business to begin operation, expand operations, or even to continue operations. Funds are needed for a variety of purposes and they must come from somewhere. The fact that funds are needed is the simple part; where they come from is another matter altogether.

This is such an important problem that if often overshadows other equally important parts of the business planning process. It is generally so obvious that a business needs financing that the majority of the early-stage effort is directed to the relief of this problem. Unfortunately, this need for financing is often resolved incorrectly out of desperation, ignorance or both. Incorrectly resolved, this aspect of your business can leave you with problems so severe that your business may never recover, and so is doomed to failure even before you start.

Even though inadequate (incorrect) financing is one of the most often identified causes of business failure, it does not need to happen this way. It is one of the easiest forms of business failure to avoid. Financing does not and must not take place apart from other aspects of your operation or as an activity separate from your business planning. In fact, financing is the heart of your enterprise and your business plan, and affects every part of your operation. It must be remembered that a good financing proposal is naturally produced in the process of creating a good business plan. The reverse, however, is frequently not true. A good business plan is far less likely to emerge out of a financing proposal. The business planning process identifies the types and amounts of financing that are required for each of the different purposes or functions of the operation. This helps to assure that the financial needs of each aspect of the business are not only considered but provided for as well. On the other hand, working backward, planning an operation around a predetermined amount of financing is not only ineffective, it is stupid. People ask, "How much money can I borrow?" The correct answer is, "How much do you need?" The business plan will provide you with an objective statement of what is going on in your business, or what you intend to have go on in your business. Take advantage of that objectivity. Small businesses have few enough fixed points to measure progress from. Your financial plan provides one of the best benchmarks possible. It automatically becomes your budget and, as your budget, the basis for your financial control system. Financing plans are expressed in dollars, and operations can also be measured in dollars to be compared against the plan.

In considering your financial needs, it is helpful to remember that there are two parties involved in any financing effort, the business seeking the financing, and the financier. Different financiers may be a bank, a professional investor, you yourself, your friends or family, different investment groups, or a variety of other individuals. A financier is simply someone who finances a business.

This is important to keep in mind because, all too often, a communication problem develops between the small business principals and their financing sources. Such problems are largely avoidable. Bankers and other professional financiers use their own jargon to evaluate loan and equity applicants. Misuse of this language creates a credibility gap; used correctly, it provides a subtle edge towards obtaining the financing you require. More importantly, understanding what is meant by this specialized language will benefit you enormously. The terminology is used here to explain the main points, generally from a banker's point of view, since bankers provide most of the small business financing. Some of the more common terms and expressions are included in the Glossary.

Another point to remember about professional lenders is that bankers and others who handle other people's money are obliged, both legally and morally, to protect their depositors' money. It is not the responsibility of these individuals, particularly bankers, to make loans. In fact, a bank is not allowed to take high risks. Accordingly, while your business ideas may sound wonderful and be highly attractive to you and your colleagues, a banker may not share your enthusiasm. If a bank does not place its depositors' funds into reasonably safe and secured investments, it violates a stringent body of law. If your deal is too risky, a bank simply cannot touch it. However, it is also helpful to remember that risk is a function of perception, and two different bankers may perceive the same situation differently. In addition, there are individuals other than bankers who may be willing to be involved with higher risk. These additional sources may include your friends and family, finance companies, or even other higher-risk organizations.

Whenever anyone considers how to finance a business the phrase "risk assessment" or some variation is likely to be discussed. Since the criteria on which risk is judged vary from businessman to banker, and you know what risk looks like from your own point of view, it may be helpful to look at risk from a banker's point of view. After all, you wouldn't be applying for financing unless you thought the risk was reasonable. The test of reasonableness is the benefit from the use of borrowed money weighed against the potential cost, cost frequently being a function of risk. Your conclusions about "reasonableness" or "risk" should not be based on "hunch" or "gut feel," but should be the result of the systematic analysis which is outlined here, and in the planning process in general.

In assessing the riskiness of a loan, a banker will generally consider at least the following:

1. Experience of the borrower: A new business is more risky than an established business. A newcomer to an industry has more danger for a banker than a well-

seasoned practitioner. Experience is one of the best business teachers. Without it, some expensive lessons are all but inevitable.

2. Experience with the borrower: The credit history of the individuals in a small company is important because loans to small businesses are, in essence, personal loans, whether they are secured or unsecured. The "character" of a person is shown with some accuracy by that person's track record. Your banker will want to know yours.
3. Ability of the borrower to pay back the loan: This is actually the single most important consideration, but it cannot be made in a vacuum. Such factors as your experience, character, the industry's cycle, and the period of the loan will all affect this part of the judgment. Your cash flow will show how the loan will be repaid. This must be clearly shown for any loan application.
4. Equity in the business: The greater the equity, the lower the risk. Bankers as a rule like to see a very low debt to worth ratio. Equity has a tendency to make people stick with their business more when it becomes troubled.
5. Collateral, cosigners and comakers: All of these reduce the risk, but, except for some finance companies, the coverage afforded by these is less important than the fact that they are tangible evidence of others' faith in your business.
6. Term of the loan: The longer the term, the higher the risk. On the other side, the shorter the term, the lower the risk. If you don't pay back a thirty-day note, your banker knows it fast. A twenty-year loan may not show problems until it is too late to cure them.

Risk assessment affects you in two direct ways, (1) whether you get the financing or not, and (2) how much the financing will cost you. By presenting your case in the best light, either through a financing plan or through a combination of plan, experience and updated statements, you enhance your chances of getting the money you need and getting it at the lowest cost. The following six-step process, if properly followed, will help you understand what kind of financing your business needs. If you take the time and trouble to follow these simple techniques, your business will be more satisfying, more successful and more profitable.

HOW TO GET FINANCING: The six steps

1. Identify different needs for funds within the business.
2. Determine how much money is needed.
3. Identify the type of money needed.
4. Schedule when the money is needed.
5. Develop a financing plan.
6. Implement and review your financing plan.

Business lending or investing bears no relationship to charity. All lenders, no matter who they are, must ask, "How will this loan be repaid?" If there is no clear answer to this question, then the loan should not be made. It's just that simple, and yet it is the difficulty of accepting this simple logic that causes an immense amount of anger and frustration on the part of small businesses who go to the money markets seeking the wrong kind of financing or inappropriate amounts, or who fail to organize and explain their ideas and objectives in a clear, straightforward way. All of these are typical errors, and all of them can be avoided.

Step 1: Identify different needs for funds within the business.

One of the most catastrophic errors small business owners make is to begin designing their business around a certain sum of dollars which they have in mind as a borrowing target. This is simply the wrong way to go. Instead, it is essential to think through the business operation and systematically evaluate how much money is needed for each of the different purposes, functions, and activities required to make this business successful. Then try to figure out whether or not it is possible or reasonable to secure that amount of financing. If it is not, then see if the plan can be scaled down to require a smaller amount of funding. If the plan can't be modified and still preserve feasibility, then forget it.

If you are starting a business, for example, you can probably list the greater portion of capital assets you will require. For most businesses, it is relatively easy to list the majority of capital assets that will be required. Included in such a list could be store fixtures, lease deposits, delivery equipment, office machinery and furniture, operating equipment, and even real estate and buildings. Study other businesses, check operating guidelines, and ask bankers or accountants. There are a variety of ways to determine the initial investments, or front-end costs, and fixed assets that are required to start your type of business adequately. The fixed assets are the capital assets and are essentially physical items. Some intangibles may creep in, such as copyrights and patents, but the physical plant and related equipment are the first parts of the business to identify and understand.

Capital assets, naturally enough, are expected to be paid for principally from invested capital or from fairly long-term loans. It is important to tie debt-life to asset-life. Short-term financial needs should be covered by short-term debt. Longer-term or capital needs generally should be covered by long-term debt or investment capital.

Suppose you are buying a company. If so, many of the costs are indeed fixed, but you should still go through the elementary calculation of determining what you need and whether you might be able to assemble the requisite resources cheaper or better in a different way. These calculations may help you to conclude that buying the business may not be such a good idea compared to starting one from scratch. This whole process, again, begins with identifying the needs of that business.

Suppose you feel you need a loan to expand. Again, you will start by identifying what your business needs, when it will be needed, and how long it will be needed for. If the financing will be in the form of debt, this planning will also help you see how you will be able to repay the loan. Then, and only then, can you begin to come up with dollar figures for the amount of financing that will be required.

Unhappily, most people invert this process. They go from trying to figure out how much money they think they can raise to trying to figure out what they could do with that money, rather than addressing the basic question of determining what business needs must be met. Ignoring this fundamental consideration is one reason so many small businesses fail. Identify the needs. Then, if you cannot finance those needs properly, you will have a better framework for trying to decide what you should do. Don't jump in before you know what you are jumping into, or you're likely to fail.

Step 2: Determine how much money is needed.

There are a variety of techniques which can be used here, but inspecting a range of costs will help you identify the boundaries of your deal. The triple approach of high/low/most-likely is worth pages of discussion in itself. It is simple. For every contemplated purchase or investment, try to identify a range of figures, one of which reflects an unlimited budget (the high), one which represents a survival budget (the low), and the most likely figure (reasonable) which is somewhere above survival but well below extravagance. (See section G, "Application and expected effect of loan or investments" in chapter 1.)

To arrive at a rough approximation of your capital needs, you must calculate the following:

1. Your capital asset cost: This includes plant, equipment, supplies, material, opening inventories, perhaps other costs as well if they are capitalized.
2. Your working capital: You must know what the maximum cumulative negative cash flow will be. This can only be determined by forecasting a cash flow projection substantially beyond the cash break-even point in order to make sure that you will have an adequate positive cash flow from your business to finance your normal operations. This will be a particularly important exercise if you are entering a period of sharp growth.
3. Your safety margin or contingency reserve: Even though we all hope that our reasonable expectations will work out, we must be prepared for them not to do so. The chances for the latter may be as good as for the former.

Your accountant or banker and others can help you with all of these, but you must be the one to provide the insight into your business. Once each of these categories has been thoughtfully examined, add them up. This will give you a rough picture of the capital you need. If anything, it may call for more capital than is absolutely necessary. This is fine. You can adjust the totals later, but the added safety factor represented by slightly overcapitalizing the operation will help you to sleep nights. The chances are that, later on, you will need to strike a balance between fixed assets and working capital, but that is another issue entirely and one that is a function of fine tuning.

Continue this approach for all other financing purposes. You begin by identifying the various needs, then place high, low, and most-likely costs against those needs. This is a good opportunity to question seriously whether or not you really need whatever it is that you're thinking about. Often you won't, but, if the need stands up and the dollar cost is not out of reach, then you are in a position once again to know, not merely guess, how much money you must raise from one source or the other to support adequately whatever the opportunity is that you want to pursue.

Step 3: Identify the type of money needed.

A series of alternatives may be available to you: debt or capital, long-term or short, secured or unsecured. Fit the financing to the purpose. The second most common financing error following undercapitalization is securing the wrong kind of financing. If the purpose of the loan is seasonal, it must be paid off seasonally. If it is stretched out to an intermediate or long-term loan, then the next year the same problem, although worse, will arise again. The obvious parallel here is to consumer debt. You start to get behind on your monthly bills, so you get a debt consolidation loan. Repayments for short-term debt are now spread over a longer term. This makes your cash flow look improved until you get deeper into debt, which will happen if you haven't changed the consumption patterns that got you into the jam in the first place. So the next step is to reconsolidate, reconsolidate again, and so forth. The hole just gets deeper and deeper, and the monthly payment bigger and bigger.

A business is no different. Recurring loan needs are best handled by a financing vehicle designed for that specific kind of need.

The other side of this problem is trying to finance long-term needs, such as fixed-asset acquisition, over a short term, perhaps by abusing a nonrevolving line of credit. This will drain off working capital quickly, and can make further growth impossible. It is also likely to destroy your ability and reputation for paying your bills and servicing your debt. If you expect to use an expensive piece of capital equipment for the next ten years, then it generally doesn't make sense to try to pay for it in six months. A term loan for some longer period of time is more likely to be the most practical solution to the problem.

Along with these other considerations, whether the financing is for debt or for capital, you must consider the cost. One reason for the repeated warning against carrying too much debt is that the cost of that money, the interest and the principal repayment, may exceed the return you can earn. This is a fine way to slowly go broke. It is almost painless until suddenly there's no working capital (except illiquid receivables) and no credit.

High debt-to-worth ratios (high leverage) can show spectacular returns on invested capital, but, if things don't work out, and they seldom do (the best laid plans . . .), then the loss figures may also be spectacular, and net worth rapidly vanishes. In most cases, banks, the Small Business Administration, and other relatively conventional lenders simply cannot lend into negative net worth situations. Generally speaking, that's the law. Too little initial capital will rapidly surface as negative net worth, and the only remedy for negative net worth is new investment.

Here is another place where your cash flow projections will be extremely useful in determining both whether you can afford whatever amount of debt you are contemplating and whether the cost is in line with the benefit. The analysis of these projections will quickly reveal the impact of different types of interest costs and repayment schedules on the operating structure of your business. Money borrowed must be repaid, generally on a monthly basis. Short-term debt borrowed for seasonal purposes must be repaid at the end of that season as the working capital cycle is completed. The new investment is put into inventories, then changed into accounts receivable, then changed into cash, which then can be used to liquidate the debt.

Your banker and accountant can help you with these considerations. You will be doubly protected, however, by looking for what kind of financing makes the most sense for you, both now and in the long run, before you go to your financing sources. Expedience will hurt you. If you follow a financially conservative path, you will do both yourself and your investors a favor.

A bit of balancing advice is appropriate here as well. Credit and debt, properly used, enable you to grow faster than an ultra-conservative no-debt strategy. Running a business but never using financing is like playing baseball but never batting. Pure defensiveness is ultimately self-defeating. Generally, you should be able to identify a middle course to run between excessiveness and ultra-conservatism. Identifying that middle course is the real challenge for all owner/managers to grapple with. Following the series of steps outlined here is a good way to come to grips with its resolution.

Step 4: Schedule when the money is needed.

It is possible to identify the timing of financing, to plan ahead, and to set specific dates. A common error in many small businesses is to leave financing needs until the last moment, that moment at which they become so pressing that a slight hitch in securing financing can seriously damage the business or even finish it off entirely.

The problem can be identified as Friday-night financing. Late on Friday afternoon, a harried business owner darts into his bank, corners his banker, and says he needs some debt money now—not Monday, but right now. Of course, the banker refuses, because one of the first lessons bankers learn is that financing in a panic is throwing money away. Such desperation is generally a sign of poor managerial judgment and a lack of planning, as well as a clear warning that a loan so hastily conceived is very likely to have an inordinately high degree of risk attached, and likely also to have no clear understanding of how or when it can be repaid.

Bankers and other lenders as well are not likely to enter risky deals. Since that is a given factor, take it into account. Once you know what kind of money and how much money is required, then and only then can you begin to set up a timetable, a plan for your financing.

For example, a line of credit for a new company may take up to six weeks to be approved, whereas a well-established company might get the same line for the same purpose over the phone. A real estate deal will almost always take a month or longer; the legalities alone will consume that time. A term loan may have to wait for an evaluation of the equipment being financed. A construction or work-in-progress loan will have a built-in timetable, but never takes less than several weeks to negotiate. And so it goes. It is necessary to visit your banker or other financiers well before you need them and to discuss the timing on the kind of loan you may require. These financiers will be happy to have such preliminary discussions with you. It is helpful for them to have you adequately fulfill your planning requirements as well. By seeing your banker before you desperately need his help, you will avoid the Friday-night financing problem.

Set the dates, then follow them. You can always slow down a loan, but it is extremely difficult to speed one up. The same holds true for equity investors, except that the time frames are likely to be longer. Getting them eager is much more difficult than discouraging them. If you know now that in a year additional capital for growth is going to be required, and that capital will not be generated from operating profits, the time to start seeking that new capital is now, before the panic sets in. Investors need time to think, and, if that time need will put you in a jam, then you will either not get the financing or the financing will be much more costly in terms of equity or control or interest or all three than it needs to be.

Step 5: Develop a financing plan.

Identify where you will secure the funds that are needed, then identify whatever actions are needed in order to make certain that you will be able to secure the needed financing. Form a backup plan and avoid problems.

Financing proposals can vary from the most thorough business plan (essential for new ventures in almost all cases) to a sketchy cash-flow and balance sheet. The amount of detail needed will naturally vary with each case. A unique or new, higher risk deal will normally need much more substantial planning and documentation than a seasonal normal order of business loan.

Part of your strategy is to make sure that you and your financing prospects keep in touch through both fat and lean times. It is important to have your financiers visit you at your place of business. This will help them develop a feel for your business in a physical way. It gives you the home-court advantage and provides them with an opportunity to offer comments on how they would run your business if it were theirs to run. This kind of advice is not only likely to be tremendously helpful, it also keeps them actively involved and actively interested in your business situation, and makes them much more likely to be responsive to you and your needs as they develop.

Your financing proposal will vary with your relationship to your sources of financing. If you are well established, you may need no more than updated financial statements and a statement of intended use and source of repayment of your debt. For a new or rapidly growing business, a more comprehensive business plan is generally necessary. As a matter of fact, this comprehensive plan should be created and updated periodically whether you need more financing from outside or not. A good business plan is a great deal of work, and it will take a lot of time, but the benefits are guaranteed to far outweigh these considerations. Either way, your aim is to keep your sources of financing favorably aware of your progress toward clearly defined business objectives. Altogether, these activities will establish your credibility with these lending sources, and credibility helps these outsiders to be sure that their needs as well as yours are being met through the financial transactions. The banker's aim is protection of his depositors' money. Therefore, he must be able to see clearly how the loan will be repaid. The investor's aim is to achieve either a satisfactory percentage return on his capital investment or to achieve a good capital gain, or both. All of you, and you as the business principal are included here as well, want to earn a return on your money that is in line with the amount of risk. A low-risk investment generally does not generate high returns. A high risk is taken in hopes of a high return. Different investors will respond to these different risk situations. It is important to keep the source of money in mind as you prepare the initial proposal, so design your arguments to suit your reader's needs.

All of this will give you a good chance of securing financing of the right kind from the right sources. However, if this primary plan fails, then you must have a backup or a contingency plan. You can't just assume that your first plan will work, so you should simultaneously begin to cultivate more than one banker, more than one finance company, factor, or investor, as the case may dictate. The basic information that you have assembled will be the same (the need, the amount, how it will be paid off), but the construction of your arguments or the discussion of your activities may differ depending on your target, and their objectives and interests.

You may find it useful to form two alternative strategies, a capital conservative plan and a more highly leveraged plan. The capital conservative plan would show that you could bootstrap your business, but would also show how this bootstrapping would constrain your growth. The more highly leveraged plan might show how the additional financing could better fuel the business's growth. Putting the two plans side by side may well encourage your banker to grant you the higher level of credit you need for maximum safe growth, rather than make him feel obliged to argue you down to a lower level of financing than you have requested, as more frequently occurs. Good management is reflected in good financial planning, and bankers respond to this key indicator of managerial competence.

Step 6: Implement and review your financing plan.

Securing and applying the financing is only the beginning. Financial planning is the basis for financial strategy, and strategy must respond to both internal and external changes in the business's environment. Good plans will rapidly become poor plans unless they are reviewed and updated periodically.

While reviewing the plan is critical, its proper implementation is even more essential. The effectiveness of your financial planning comes through its application in the manner intended. In other words, make sure that the funds are being used according to the plan unless a better use is revealed as your operation begins to develop—not a more pressing use, but a better use. It is easy to mistake loan proceeds for operating profits, and many (bankrupt) businesses have fallen into this trap. You have made your plan based on solid business considerations. The key to success, however, is to follow it. This is a trap well worth reacknowledging. Good plans are made, appropriate financing is secured, and then the owner suddenly decides to buy a few other things, originally unintended, for the business as well. If the funds have been secured for working capital purposes, for instance, they must be saved for that purpose. Good plans are made in a perfectly logical fashion. The trouble comes from suddenly having a large amount of money available. Often, emotion of the moment takes over and the logic of the plan is set aside. This is a not uncommon occurrence which results from the business owner suddenly having at his disposal more cash than he has ever had under his control before. The consequences that follow imprudence at this point are likely to be disastrous.

Since your financing needs are likely to be ongoing, and will continue to be if you stay in business and grow, your plan should be reviewed by both you and your financiers at least annually, and preferably more often. There is a built-in bonus in all of this. Once formulated, your financing plan becomes an integral part of your budget/control process. Using your plan in this manner, you will be tuned to changes in your environment, both negative and positive, and will be able to respond to these changes to your maximum benefit.

Summary

By carefully analyzing your financing needs and expressing them in an objective way (see Figure 6-1), you avoid problems caused by inadequate capitalization, excessive debt, poor use of the powerful tool of credit (both trade and other debt), and Friday-night financing. Good financial management follows from a clear understanding of how and why money takes different shapes and fills different purposes in your business. Good financial management is the cornerstone for better, more satisfying, and more profitable business operations.

Figure 6-1. Analytical chart for financing plan

Financing Needed	Type of Financing																
	Equity (personal)	Equity (other)	Long-term debt	Mortgage	Secured	Unsecured	Intermediate-term debt	Short-term debt	A/R financing	Field warehousing	Unsecured	Personal	A/R factoring	Line of credit	Accounts payable	Floor planning	Second mortgage
Start-up																	
Organizational expenses (legal, deposits, dev.)	1, 14	2	5, 11				5, 11					14					
Initial inventory	1	2	5, 11				5, 11										
Capital expenditures																	
Plant/real estate	1	2, 12 13		6, 10 11	7												
Equipment	1	2, 12 13			5, 7 8, 10												
Fixtures	1	2				5, 11	5, 11										
Working capital	1	2				5, 11	5, 11	5,11				14					
Seasonal																	
Inventory								5,11		1, 7		14		5, 11	3	7	
Accounts receivable									5, 7 9				5, 7 9				
Payroll/supplies											5, 11	14		5, 11			
Marketing											5, 11	14		5, 11			
Growth																	
Inventory	1, 4	2			7	5, 11											9, 14
Equipment	1, 4	2, 12 13			7, 8 5, 11	5, 11											9, 14
Physical improvements	1, 4	2		6	5, 11		5, 11										9, 14
Working capital	1, 4	2					5, 11										9, 14

SOURCES OF FINANCING

1. Owners, relatives, friends
2. Private investors
3. Trade credit
4. Profits
5. Commercial banks
6. Savings banks
7. Commercial credit companies
8. Leasing companies
9. Finance companies
10. Life insurance companies
11. S. B. A.
12. S. B. I. C.'s
13. L. D. C.'s
14. Consumer finance companies

Part III.
A SAMPLE BUSINESS PLAN

FINANCING PROPOSAL FOR

FINESTKIND SEAFOODS, INC.

FINANCING PROPOSAL

FOR

FINESTKIND SEAFOODS, INC.

To be Submitted To

The Great Bay Bank & Trust Co.

and

The Small Business Administration

Mike Gosling
Mike Swan
123 Fish Lane
Port Lobster, N.H. 03899
603-436-6218

October 31, 19-

Statement of Purpose

Finestkinds Seafoods, Inc. is seeking a loan of $36,000 to purchase equipment and inventory, purchase property and buildings at 123 Fish Lane, Port Lobster, N.H., perform necessary renovations and improvements, maintain sufficient cash reserves, and provide adequate working capital to successfully expand an existing wholesale/retail seafood market. This sum, together with the $10,000 equity investment of the principals, will be sufficient to finance transition through the expansion phase so this recently started business can operate as an ongoing, profitable enterprise.

Table of Contents

I. The Business

Description

Finestkind Seafoods, Inc. is a fish market specializing in selling extremely fresh (no more than one day from the boat) seafood to both retail and wholesale customers. At present, 60 percent of sales are to retail customers. Finestkind Seafoods plans to concentrate more heavily on the wholesale trade (restaurants and grocery chains) in the future. Our experience has shown that even though the markup is lower for wholesale trade, profits are higher due to lower personnel costs and faster turnover of inventory.

Finestkind Seafoods, Inc. began business in September, 19- and is open seven days a week from 10:00 a.m. to 8:30 p.m. for retail business and from 6:00 a.m. to 8:30 p.m. for wholesale. The retail demand is seasonal and fluctuates according to the weather (our store is located on a tourist route). The wholesale demand is constant and increasing. We feel that the latter can be improved by more direct selling. Our customers agree (see letters from Nightlife Clambake and Grandiose Superettes in the supporting documents). The quality of our seafood is exceptional, and since Mr. Swan is a former fisherman with many personal friends in the fishing industry, we do not anticipate difficulty maintaining good relations with our suppliers. We have made a policy of paying premium prices in cash at dockside for the best, freshest fish.

Market

Finestkind Seafoods, Inc. will continue to provide premium quality seafoods to both wholesale (restaurants and markets) and retail customers, emphasizing the former. Our goal is to provide the freshest seafood at competitive prices to customers within twenty-five miles of Port Lobster. This market has a total population of over 100,000 people (see excerpt from the census report in the supporting documents), and a potential of 300 wholesale customers. Customers will be attracted by: (1) direct approach to restaurants and markets; (2) a local radio and newspaper advertising campaign; (3) word-of-mouth advertising from our current customer base, and (4) our location on a heavily traveled tourist-route.

-1-

Competition

There are three seafood operations directly competing with Finestkind Seafoods.

1. Ferd's Fish--scattered operation with one truck making the rounds and a small counter leased from a supermarket in Pig Gut Village. We have cut into their sales by making promised deliveries on time and at the agreed price. As a result, their operation has become marginal.

2. Kingfisher--clean, three-man operation specializing in cheaper fish. Have trouble with their suppliers because they aren't willing to pay top, dockside prices. Otherwise, sell directly to housewives from a fleet of three trucks, have some wholesale trade which they hope to expand. Their sales are apparently expanding because they have been serving the same routes for five years and have an excellent reputation. Located in Rye.

3. Jonah's Seafoods--good relations with suppliers, has most of the supermarket trade, no retail. Currently rebuilding due to disastrous fire but will be our most serious competition when his new store opens. Twenty-five years of experience in the Pig Gut/Port Lobster area, good location on scenic bridge over Pig Gut Inlet two miles south of Finestkind on tourist route; plans to open retail store and may be willing to give up part of wholesale since he is getting on in years.

The indirect competition is from the major processors in Portland (forty-five miles east) and Boston (sixty miles south). Since we fall between their primary market areas, we can purchase from both on a consignment basis.

Location

Finestkind is currently leasing a one-story, wooden-frame building with cement floor (2,000 square feet) at 123 Fish Lane, Port Lobster, New Hampshire for $175 per month with an option to buy at $22,000 (in writing). The area is zoned for commercial use. Fish Lane is part of U.S. Route 1, a heavily traveled tourist route with most businesses nearby catering to the tourist trade. Finestkind has performed major leasehold improvements including a walk-in freezer and rough-sawn, pine-board walls. The building is divided into: (1) sales/counter area (1,200 square feet); (2) cutting area (100 square feet); and (3) other--space for toilet, potential storage and/or sales area totaling 700 square feet. See diagram included in supporting documents.

Management

Mr. Gosling was born in Port Lobster and has lived there all his life. After graduating from Port Lobster schools and serving in the US Navy for three years, he became a self-employed carpenter, taking night courses in small-business management and sales at Pig Gut State, with the ultimate aim of owning and managing a retail store. He also serves as a member of the zoning board for Port Lobster. He and his wife (a medical secretary) live in Port Lobster with their two children.

Mr. Swan was born in Zilch, Wisconsin, in 1950, attended schools in Utah, Alaska, and Florida, and served four years in the Marines (rank upon separation, E-3). He test-drove motorcycles for a year, then served as Parts Manager for Wheely Cycles, Inc., before joining the Fatback Fishfood division of Grandiose Foodstuff, Inc. as a packer in March 1973 in their East Machias, Maine plant. In June 1975, he resigned as line foreman of the Frozen Food Filleting Department to join Mr. Gosling in the Finestkind operation. He is unmarried and lives in Pig Gut.

Both men are healthy and energetic; they believe their abilities complement each other and will permit them to make Finestkind a success. In particular, Mr. Swan knows all of the fishermen, while Mr. Gosling is well known by the entire community. Since Mr. Swan has had experience in cost control and line management, he will be responsible for the store and inventory control. Mr. Gosling will be primarily responsible for the development of the wholesale business and, with Mr. Swan, will set policy. Personnel decisions will be made jointly.

Salaries will be $215/month for the first year to enable the business to pay off start-up costs. (Mr. Gosling's wife earns enough to support his family; Mr. Swan's personal expenditures are very low since he shares a house with five other unmarried men.) In the second year, they will earn $600/month; in the third year $660/month, with any profit returned to the business.

In order to augment their skills, Mr. Gosling and Mr. Swan have enlisted the help of Scrooge Farley, CPA, and Mason Petrocelli, Esq. Other potential resources have been located and spoken with, including the Port Lobster Business Information Center (Andrew O'Bangfo), Pig Gut State's Venture Incubator Division (Dr. Good), the Smaller Business Association of New England, and the Fish Retailers Organized for Growth (FROG). Marshall Sailor, a retired Port Lobster banker, has agreed to serve on the Finestkind board and will provide ongoing management review. Other members of the board are Farley, Petrocelli, Gosling, and Swan.

Personnel

Finestkind will hire one part-time salesperson within six months whose duties will be selling seafoods over the counter to the retail customers. He or she will be paid the minimum wage ($2.30/hour) for weekend work; no fringe benefits or overtime are anticipated. We will also employ, on an as-needed basis, one cutter at $3.75/hour to help prepare seafood for the wholesale trade.

Application and Expected Effect of Loan

The $36,000 will be used as follows:

Purchase of 123 Fish Lane property	$22,000
Equipment: '7X Ford P/U with insulated body	1,885
Dayton compressor (used, serial #45-cah-990)	115
Sharp Slicer (used, Speedy model)	200
Renovations (see contractor's letter in supporting documents)	4,000
Working capital	4,000
Inventory	500
Reserve (not disbursed)	3,300
Total	$36,000

Finestkind Seafoods, Inc. can purchase the 123 Fish Lane property at a substantial saving under terms of the lease/purchase agreement signed July, 19-. An independent appraiser has calculated the value of the property, including leasehold improvements by Finestkind, at $30,000. The monthly payment for a twelve-year mortage will be $250/month, a net increase of $75/month over the current rent. See Financial Data for the effect on the business.

The truck will be used to deliver merchandise to our wholesale customers, retard spoilage, and maintain the quality of our merchandise.

The compressor will replace the compressor now used for our refrigeration unit and should lower electric costs.

The slicer will eliminate four man-hours of work daily. The time released will be used for soliciting more business and processing a greater volume of whole fish. With the slicer, relatively untrained help can fillet flounder with minimal waste.

The renovations are: a deep well (water) required by the state, a toilet and wash sink separate from the work area, and replacement of the current, obsolete heating system, which will reduce fuel expense.

The working capital will enable Finestkind to meet current expenses, offset negative (seasonal) cash flow as shown in the Working Capital Analysis in Financial Data, and insure the continued growth of the business.

The inventory is to take advantage of bulk rates on certain fresh-frozen packaged goods (baitfish, South African lobster tails).

The reserve will be held by the bank as a line of credit to be used to take advantage of special opportunities or to meet emergencies.

Summary

Finestkind Seafoods, Inc. is a fish market serving both retail and wholesale markets in and around Port Lobster, New Hampshire. Mike Gosling and Mike Swan, the owners, are seeking $36,000 to purchase the building at 123 Fish Lane, perform necessary renovations and improvements to the property, maintain cash reserves, and provide adequate working capital. This amount will be sufficient to finance transition through a planned expansion phase so the business can operate as an ongoing profitable venture.

Careful analysis of the potential market shows an unfilled demand for exceptionally fresh seafood. Mr. Gosling's local reputation will help secure a sizeable portion of the wholesale market, while Mr. Swan's managerial experience assures that the entire operation will be carefully controlled. In addition to a working board, Mr. Gosling's studies at Pig Gut State will provide even more control over the projected growth of Finestkind.

The funds sought will result in a greater increase in fixed assets than may be shown, as Mr. Gosling will be performing much of the renovation and improvements himself. The additional reserve and working capital will enable Finestkind to substantially increase its sales while maintaining profitability.

II. FINANCIAL DATA

Finestkind Seafoods, Inc.

Sources and Applications of Funding

Sources		
Bank Loans:		
1. Mortage loan	$22,000	
2. Term loan	10,700	
3. Reserved loan	3,300	
4. Owners' investment	5,000	
Total		$41,000
Applications		
Purchase building	$22,000	
Equipment	2,200	
Renovations	4,000	
Inventory	500	
Working capital	4,000	
Reserve for contingencies	8,300	
Total		$41,000

To be secured

by

Assets of the Business
Signatures of the Principles

Mike Gosling

Mike Swan

SBA Guarantee

Finestkind Seafoods, Inc.
Capital Equipment List

Major Equipment and Normal Accessories	Model	Cost or List Price (Lower)
Storequip, Inc., display case, glass front, refrigerated	Handmade	$ 200
Storequip, Inc., display case, glass front, ice	SST6-77K	400
Dayton air compressor	#45-cah-990	115
Bendix standing freezer	3979-7584	125
Nameless, Inc., standard freezer	--	50
Cleaning table, fibreglassed	Handmade	200
Freezing locker and compressor	Handmade	3,000
Total		$4,090
Minor Shop Equipment		
Miscellaneous knives, scalers, etc.	--	$ 75
Miscellaneous display trays, storage boxes	--	50
Total		$ 125
Other Equipment		
Pickup truck with insulated body	19- Ford, Lo-Bed	$1,885
Safe	1879 Mosler	100
Cash register	523 NCR	50
Calculator	TI-120	65
Light fixture	Custom design	100
Total		$2,200
Total capital equipment		$6,415

Finestkind Seafoods, Inc.

Pro Forma

Balance Sheet

October 15, 19-

Assets		Liabilities and Net Worth	
Current assets:		Current Liabilities:	
Cash	$ 530	Accounts payable	$2,077
Accounts receivable (net)	100	Current portion LTD	1,440
Merchandise inventory	700	Total current liabilities	$3,517
Supplies	175		
Prepaid expenses	80	Long-term liabilities:	
Total current assets	$1,585	Notes payable (a)	$ 535
Fixed assets:		Bank loan payable (b)	1,360
Fixtures and leasehold improvements	$3,750	Equity loan payable (c)	1,250
Building (freezer)	3,000	Total long-term liabilities	$3,145
Equipment	1,100		
Trucks	2,500	Total liabilities	$6,662
Total fixed assets	$10,350	Net worth owners' equity	$5,273
Total assets	$11,935	Total liabilities and net worth	$11,935

Accounts payable display:		
	Eldridge's, Inc.	$1,700
	Lesswing's	119
	Paxtone	180
	Pig Gut Reefer	78
		$2,077

(a) Dave N. Hall for electrical work
(b) Term loan secured by '64 Jeep, "71 Ford
(c) S & C Greed Finance Corp., Pig Gut, N.H.

-9-

Break-even Analysis

Fixed costs = \$14,700
Variable costs = 79.3%
Gross margin = 20.7%

Thus, BE = FC ÷ GM

$$BE = \frac{\$14,700}{.207}$$

BE = \$71,014.50
BE/month = \$ 5,917.87

Calculation for sales needed per month at break-even

Average unit selling price	=	\$ 3.00
Average customer repeat sales = 2X/week	=	6.00
4.3 weeks/month; thus, average customer sale/month	=	25.80
Thus, customers needed at BE	=	230/month
	=	7.6/day

Break-even Analysis for First Operating Year (from income projections, following pages)

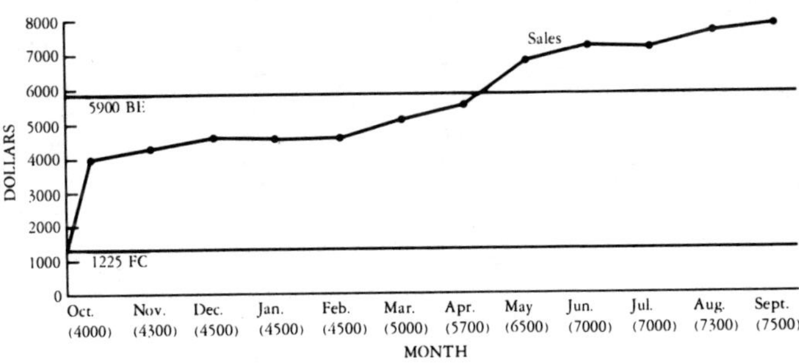

-10-

Finestkind Seafoods, Inc.

Income Projection

Pro Forma Profit and Loss

Three-Year Summary

	Year 1	Year 2	Year 3
Sales			
Wholesale	$27,400	$ 68,800	$ 84,000
Retail	40,400	91,000	91,000
Total sales	67,800	159,800	175,000
Cost of material	52,884	124,625	136,550
Variable labor cost	900	3,250	5,200
Cost of goods sold	53,784	127,875	141,750
Gross margin	14,016	31,925	33,250
Operating expenses:			
Utilities	1,200	1,680	1,920
Salaries	5,160	14,400	16,000
Payroll taxes and benefits	480	1,360	1,360
Advertising	480	720	720
Office supplies	120	180	180
Insurance	600	600	600
Maintenance and cleaning	240	300	300
Legal and accounting	500	740	740
Delivery expense	1,320	1,802	1,764
Licenses	60	60	60
Boxes, paper, etc.	120	240	240
Telephone	600	720	720
Depreciation	480	480	840
Miscellaneous	275	400	400
Total operating expense	11,635	23,682	25,844
Other expenses:			
Interest (mortage) 9.75%	2,160	2,160	2,160
Interest (loan) 10.75%	900	900	900
Total other expenses	3,060	3,060	3,060
Total expenses	14,695	26,742	28,904
Net profit (loss) pre-tax	$ (684)	$ 5,183	$ 4,346 *

* Net profit is down slightly because of an increase in salaries paid to the two partners.

Income Projections
Finestkind Seafoods, Inc.
October 19-- to September 19--

	Oct. 19-	Nov. 19-	Dec. 19-	Jan. 19-	Feb. 19-	Mar. 19-	Apr. 19-	May 19-	June 19-	July 19-	Aug. 19-	Sept. 19-	Total
Sales													
Wholesale	1,000	1,200	1,400	1,600	1,800	2,200	2,400	2,800	3,100	3,100	3,300	3,500	27,400
Retail	3,000	3,100	3,100	2,900	2,700	2,800	3,300	3,700	3,900	3,900	4,000	4,000	40,400
Total sales	4,000	4,300	4,500	4,500	4,500	5,000	5,700	6,500	7,000	7,000	7,300	7,500	67,800
Cost of material	3,120	3,354	3,510	3,510	3,510	3,900	4,446	5,070	5,460	5,460	5,694	5,850	52,884
Variable labor cost								200	200	200	200	100	900
Cost of goods sold	3,120	3,354	3,510	3,510	3,510	3,900	4,446	5,270	5,660	5,660	5,894	5,950	53,784
Gross margin	880	946	990	990	990	1,100	1,254	1,230	1,340	1,340	1,406	1,550	14,016
Operating expenses													
Utilities	100	100	100	100	100	100	100	100	100	100	100	100	1,200
Salaries	430	430	430	430	430	430	430	430	430	430	430	430	5,160
Payroll taxes and benefits	40	40	40	40	40	40	40	40	40	40	40	40	480
Advertising	40	40	40	40	40	40	40	40	40	40	40	40	480
Office supplies	10	10	10	10	10	10	10	10	10	10	10	10	120
Insurance	50	50	50	50	50	50	50	50	50	50	50	50	600
Maintenance and cleaning	20	20	20	20	20	20	20	20	20	20	20	20	240
Legal and accounting	42	42	42	42	42	42	42	42	42	42	42	42	504
Delivery expense	110	110	110	110	110	110	110	110	110	110	110	110	1,320
Licenses	5	5	5	5	5	5	5	5	5	5	5	5	60
Boxes, paper, etc.	10	10	10	10	10	10	10	10	10	10	10	10	120
Telephone	50	50	50	50	50	50	50	50	50	50	50	50	600
Depreciation	40	40	40	40	40	40	40	40	40	40	40	40	480
Miscellaneous	23	23	23	23	23	23	23	23	23	23	23	23	276
Total operating expense	970	970	970	970	970	970	970	970	970	970	970	970	11,640
Other expenses:													
Interest (mortgage) 9.75%	180	180	180	180	180	180	180	180	180	180	180	180	2,160
Interest (loan) 10.75%	75	75	75	75	75	75	75	75	75	75	75	75	900
Total other expenses	255	255	255	255	255	255	255	255	255	255	255	255	3,060
Total all expenses	1,225	1,225	1,225	1,225	1,225	1,225	1,225	1,225	1,225	1,225	1,225	1,225	14,700
Net profit (loss) pre-tax	(345)	(279)	(235)	(235)	(235)	(125)	29	5	115	115	181	325	(684)
Taxes	—	—	—	—	—	—	—	—	—	—	—	—	—
Net profit (loss)	—	—	—	—	—	—	—	—	—	—	—	—	—

Income Projections
Finestkind Seafoods, Inc.
By Quarters, Years 2 and 3

	1st qtr Year 2 (Dec)	2nd qtr Year 2 (Mar)	3rd qtr Year 2 (Jun)	4th qtr Year 2 (Sept)	Total Year 2	1st qtr Year 3 (Dec)	2nd qtr Year 3 (Mar)	3rd qtr Year 3 (Jun)	4th qtr Year 3 (Sept)	Total Year 3
Sales										
Wholesale	14,800	16,000	18,000	20,000	68,800	18,000	20,000	22,000	24,000	84,000
Retail	21,000	21,000	22,000	27,000	91,000	21,000	21,000	22,000	27,000	91,000
Total sales	35,800	37,000	40,000	47,000	159,800	39,000	41,000	44,000	51,000	175,000
Cost of material	27,925	28,850	31,200	36,650	124,625	30,450	32,000	34,300	39,800	136,550
Variable labor cost	750	750	750	1,000	3,250	1,000	1,200	1,500	1,500	5,200
Cost of goods sold	28,675	29,600	31,950	37,650	127,875	31,450	33,200	35,800	41,300	141,750
Gross margin	7,125	7,400	8,050	9,350	31,925	7,550	7,800	8,200	9,700	33,250
Operating expenses										
Utilities	420	420	420	420	1,680	480	480	480	480	1,920
Salaries	3,600	3,600	3,600	3,600	14,400	4,000	4,000	4,000	4,000	16,000
Payroll taxes and benefits	340	340	340	340	1,360	380	380	380	380	1,520
Advertising	180	180	180	180	720	180	180	180	180	720
Office supplies	45	45	45	45	180	45	45	45	45	180
Insurance	150	150	150	150	600	150	150	150	150	600
Maintenance and cleaning	75	75	75	75	300	75	75	75	75	300
Legal and accounting	185	185	185	185	740	185	185	185	185	740
Delivery expense	387	420	471	524	1,802	378	420	462	504	1,764
Licenses	15	15	15	15	60	15	15	15	15	60
Boxes, paper, etc.	60	60	60	60	240	60	60	60	60	240
Telephone	180	180	180	180	720	180	180	180	180	720
Depreciation	120	120	120	120	480	120	120	120	120	480
Miscellaneous	100	100	100	100	400	100	100	100	100	400
Total operating expense	5,857	5,890	5,941	5,994	23,682	6,348	6,390	6,432	6,474	25,644
Other expenses:										
Interest (mortgage)	540	540	540	540	2,160	540	540	540	540	2,160
Interest (loan)	225	225	225	225	900	225	225	225	225	900
Total other expenses	765	765	765	765	3,060	765	765	765	765	3,060
Total all expenses	6,622	6,655	6,706	6,759	26,742	7,113	7,155	7,197	7,239	28,704
Net profit (loss) pre-tax	440	715	1,365	2,665	5,183	437	645	1,003	2,461	4,546
Taxes	—	—	—	—	—	—	—	—	—	—
Net profit (loss)	—	—	—	—	—	—	—	—	—	—

Notes of Explanation

for

Finestkind Seafoods, Inc. Income Projections

1. Sales: Includes sales of seafood and sales of ancillary products (seasonings, sauces, baitbags, bait).

2. Finestkind plans to service the wholesale trade more extensively than is shown here, although the trend has been built into the projection. Retail sales are expected to be more volatile than wholesale, leveling off at a capacity of $9,000/month due to space restrictions. The volatility is due to seasonal traffic, which builds up from late March to the late summer peak. The increase shown in the wholesale trade (2) is based on both the greater number of restaurants open in the summer and the intensive effort planned for the winter months, to sell directly to the many restaurants to which Finestkind has not yet introduced their product. Sales for September 19- were $5,450; so these figures are very conservative.

3. Cost of material: Finestkind's inventory has an average cost of 70 percent of sales (including a start-up spoilage rate of 5 percent which has been reduced to under 1 percent of sales), and has been calculated as 78 percent of sales to allow for the fluctuation of dockside fish prices during the winter.

4. Variable labor cost: One part-time counter helper for summer weekends and one part-time cutter to help prepare seafood for restaurant trade at peak times.

5. Utilities: Prorated by agreement with the utility companies involved. The expected prorated figure is $90/month, but it may increase.

6. Salaries: $50/week for each principal. This is an extremely low figure to which the principals have agreed in order to build up their business.

7. Payroll taxes and benefits: 9.5% of item (14).

8. Advertising: Local newspaper and radio spots. It is believed that a consistent, though modest, campaign will be more productive than a sporadically intensive campaign.

9. Insurance: Includes liability, key-man disability, and life.

10. Maintenance and cleaning: Mainly supplies. A market such as this must meet stringent health codes.

11. Legal and accounting: Retainers to Mason Petrocelli, Esq. and Scrooge Farley, CPA.

12. Delivery expense: Delivery of merchandise to restaurants and other markets.

13. Licenses: Required by state and municipality.

14. Boxes, paper, etc.: Packaging supplies.

15. Telephone: Needed for sales, pricing, contacting both suppliers and market.

16. Depreciation: Accountant's figure for depreciation of plant and equipment.

17. Miscellaneous: Operating expenses too small to be itemized.

18. Interest (mortage): $22,000 at 9.5 percent for fifteen years.

19. Interest (loan): $8,500 at 10.75 percent for seven years.

pro forma cash flow* detailed by month for first year

Finestkind Seafoods, Inc.
October 19- to September 19-

	Oct. 19-	Nov. 19-	Dec. 19-	Jan. 19-	Feb. 19-	Mar. 19-	Apr. 19-	May 19-	June 19-	July 19-	Aug. 19-	Sept. 19-	Total
Cash receipts													
Income from sales													
Wholesale	1,000	1,200	1,400	1,600	1,800	2,200	2,400	2,800	3,100	3,100	3,300	3,500	27,400
Retail	3,000	3,100	3,100	2,900	2,700	2,800	3,300	3,700	3,900	3,900	4,000	4,000	40,400
Total cash receipts	4,000	4,300	4,500	4,500	4,500	5,000	5,700	6,500	7,000	7,000	7,300	7,500	67,800
Cash disbursements													
Cost of goods	3,120	3,354	3,510	3,510	3,510	3,900	4,446	5,070	5,460	5,460	5,694	5,850	52,884
Variable labor								200	200	200	200	100	900
Advertising	100	25	25	25	25	40	40	40	40	40	40	40	480
Insurance			150			150			150			150	600
Legal and accounting		125			125			125			125		500
Delivery expense	80	85	90	95	100	110	110	120	130	130	135	135	1,320
Fixed cash disbursements	688	688	688	688	688	688	688	688	688	688	688	688	8,256
Loan #1	45	145	145	145	145	145	145	145	145	145	145	145	1,740
Mortgage	250	250	250	250	250	250	250	250	250	250	250	250	3,000
Total cash disbursements	4,383	4,672	4,858	4,713	4,843	5,283	5,679	6,638	7,063	6,913	7,277	7,358	69,680
Net cash flow	(383)	(372)	(358)	(213)	(343)	(283)	21	(138)	(63)	87	23	142	(1,880)
Cumulative cash flow	(383)	(755)	(1,113)	(1,326)	(1,669)	(1,952)	(1,931)	(2,069)	(2,132)	(2,045)	(2,022)	(1,880)	
Cash on hand: Loan proc.	4,000												
Cash	533												
Opening balance	4,533	4,152	3,780	3,422	3,209	2,866	2,583	2,604	2,466	2,403	2,490	2,513	
Plus cash receipts	4,000	4,300	4,500	4,500	4,500	5,000	5,700	6,500	7,000	7,000	7,300	7,500	
Less cash disbursements	4,383	4,672	4,858	4,713	4,843	5,283	5,679	6,638	7,063	6,913	7,277	7,358	
Total new balance	4,152	3,780	3,422	3,209	2,866	2,583	2,604	2,466	2,403	2,490	2,513	2,655	

Fixed cash disbursements	
Utilities	100
Salaries	430
Payroll taxes and benefits	40
Office supplies	10
Maintenance and cleaning	20
Licenses	5
Boxes, paper, etc.	10
Telephone	50
Miscellaneous	23
	688

*Assuming $8,500 loan and $22,000 mortgage loan.

pro forma cash flow detailed by quarter for second and third years

Finestkind Seafoods, Inc.
By Quarters for Years 2 and 3

	1st qtr Year 2 (Dec)	2nd qtr Year 2 (Mar)	3rd qtr Year 2 (Jun)	4th qtr Year 2 (Sept)	Total Year 2	1st qtr Year 3 (Dec)	2nd qtr Year 3 (Mar)	3rd qtr Year 3 (Jun)	4th qtr Year 3 (Sept)	Total Year 3
Cash receipts										
Income from sales										
Wholesale	14,800	16,000	18,000	20,000	68,800	18,000	20,000	22,000	24,000	84,000
Retail	21,000	21,000	22,000	27,000	91,000	21,000	21,000	22,000	27,000	91,000
Total cash receipts	35,800	37,000	40,000	47,000	159,800	39,000	41,000	44,000	51,000	175,000
Cash disbursements										
Cost of goods	27,925	28,850	31,200	36,650	124,625	30,450	32,000	34,300	39,800	136,550
Variable labor	750	750	750	1,000	3,250	1,000	1,200	1,500	1,500	5,200
Advertising	180	180	180	180	720	180	180	180	180	720
Insurance	150	150	150	150	600	150	150	150	150	600
Legal and accounting	185	185	185	185	740	185	185	185	185	740
Delivery expense	387	420	471	524	1,802	378	420	462	504	1,764
Fixed cash disbursements	4,772	4,805	4,856	4,909	19,342	5,263	5,305	5,347	5,389	21,304
Loan #1	435	435	435	435	1,740	435	435	435	435	1,740
Mortgage	750	750	750	750	3,000	750	750	750	750	3,000
Total cash disbursements	35,534	36,525	38,977	44,783	155,819	38,791	40,625	43,309	48,893	171,618
Net cash flow	266	475	1,023	2,217	3,981	209	375	691	2,107	3,382
Cumulative cash flow	266	741	1,764	3,981			584	1,275	3,382	

Fixed cash disbursements	Year 2	Year 3
Utilities	140	160
Salaries	1200	1333
Payroll taxes and benefits	113	126
Office supplies	15	15
Maintenance and cleaning	25	25
Licenses	5	5
Boxes, paper, etc.	20	20
Telephone	60	60
Miscellaneous	33	33
Total fixed cash disbursements	4835	5335

Notes of Explanation

for

Finestkind Seafoods, Inc. Pro Forma Cash Flow

1. Wholesale: See income projection for derivation of these figures.

2. Retail: See income projection for derivation of these figures.

3. Cost of goods: 78 percent of line 5.

4. Variable labor: $200/month from May to mid-September to handle the extra tourist traffic on weekends and extra seafood preparation costs associated with two restaurants which do weekend clambakes during peak season.

5. Advertising: $100 for initial burst, $25/month thereafter.

6. Insurance: Payable quarterly.

7. Legal and accounting: Retainers payable quarterly.

8. Delivery expense: Projected to increase less slowly than wholesale sales due to careful route planning.

9. Loan #1: $8,500 SBA guaranteed loan at 10.75 percent for seven years.

10. Mortage: $22,000 at 9.5 percent for fifteen years.

III. SUPPORTING DOCUMENTS

NIGHTLIFE CLAMBAKES
222 Rural Lane
Pig Gut & Port Lobster

September 10, 19-

Gentlemen:

It is a pleasure to write this letter of recommendation for Finestkind Seafoods, Inc. Our dealings with Messrs. Gosling and Swan have been completely satisfactory. Our business requires a dependable supply of fresh fish, clams, and lobsters of first quality. We have consistently received seafood products from Finestkind which meet these standards.

Our business is growing and we look forward to an ongoing relationship with Finestkind to satisfy our needs and customers.

Yours,

Donald Duck

General Characteristics of the Population: 1970

Census Tracts	SMSA
RACE	
All persons	**113 408**
White	112 266
Negro	821
Percent Negro	0.7
AGE BY SEX	
Male, all ages	**55 573**
Under 5 years	6 136
3 and 4 years	2 676
5 to 9 years	7 293
5 years	1 435
6 years	1 440
10 to 14 years	7 123
14 years	1 352
15 to 19 years	5 036
15 years	1 247
16 years	1 204
17 years	1 109
18 years	851
19 years	625
20 to 24 years	2 797
20 years	551
21 years	526
25 to 34 years	7 074
35 to 44 years	7 112
45 to 54 years	5 935
55 to 59 years	2 132
60 to 64 years	1 620
65 to 74 years	2 068
75 years and over	1 247
Female, all ages	**57 835**
Under 5 years	5 849
3 and 4 years	2 530
5 to 9 years	7 086
5 years	1 397
6 years	1 404
10 to 14 years	6 671
14 years	1 212
15 to 19 years	4 955
15 years	1 211
16 years	1 172
17 years	1 083
18 years	814
19 years	675
20 to 24 years	3 103
20 years	582
21 years	532
25 to 34 years	7 774
35 to 44 years	7 097
45 to 54 years	6 096
55 to 59 years	2 213
60 to 64 years	1 932
65 to 74 years	2 896
75 years and over	2 163
RELATIONSHIP TO HEAD OF HOUSEHOLD	
All persons	**113 408**
In households	112 270
Head of household	30 616
Head of family	26 930
Primary individual	3 686
Wife of head	24 214
Other relative of head	56 373
Not related to head	1 067
In group quarters	1 138
Persons per household	3.67
TYPE OF FAMILY AND NUMBER OF OWN CHILDREN	
All families	**26 930**
With own children under 18 years	17 535
Number of children	45 625
Husband-wife families	**24 214**
With own children under 18 years	16 236
Number of children	42 503
Percent of total under 18 years	90.1
Families with other male head	**516**
With own children under 18 years	150
Number of children	317
Families with female head	**2 200**
With own children under 18 years	1 149
Number of children	2 805
Percent of total under 18 years	5.9
Persons under 18 years	47 184
MARITAL STATUS	
Male, 14 years old and over	**36 373**
Single	9 822
Married	25 166
Separated	312
Widowed	861
Divorced	524
Female, 14 years old and over	**39 441**
Single	8 997
Married	25 465
Separated	560
Widowed	3 973
Divorced	1 006

P—2

CENSUS TRACTS

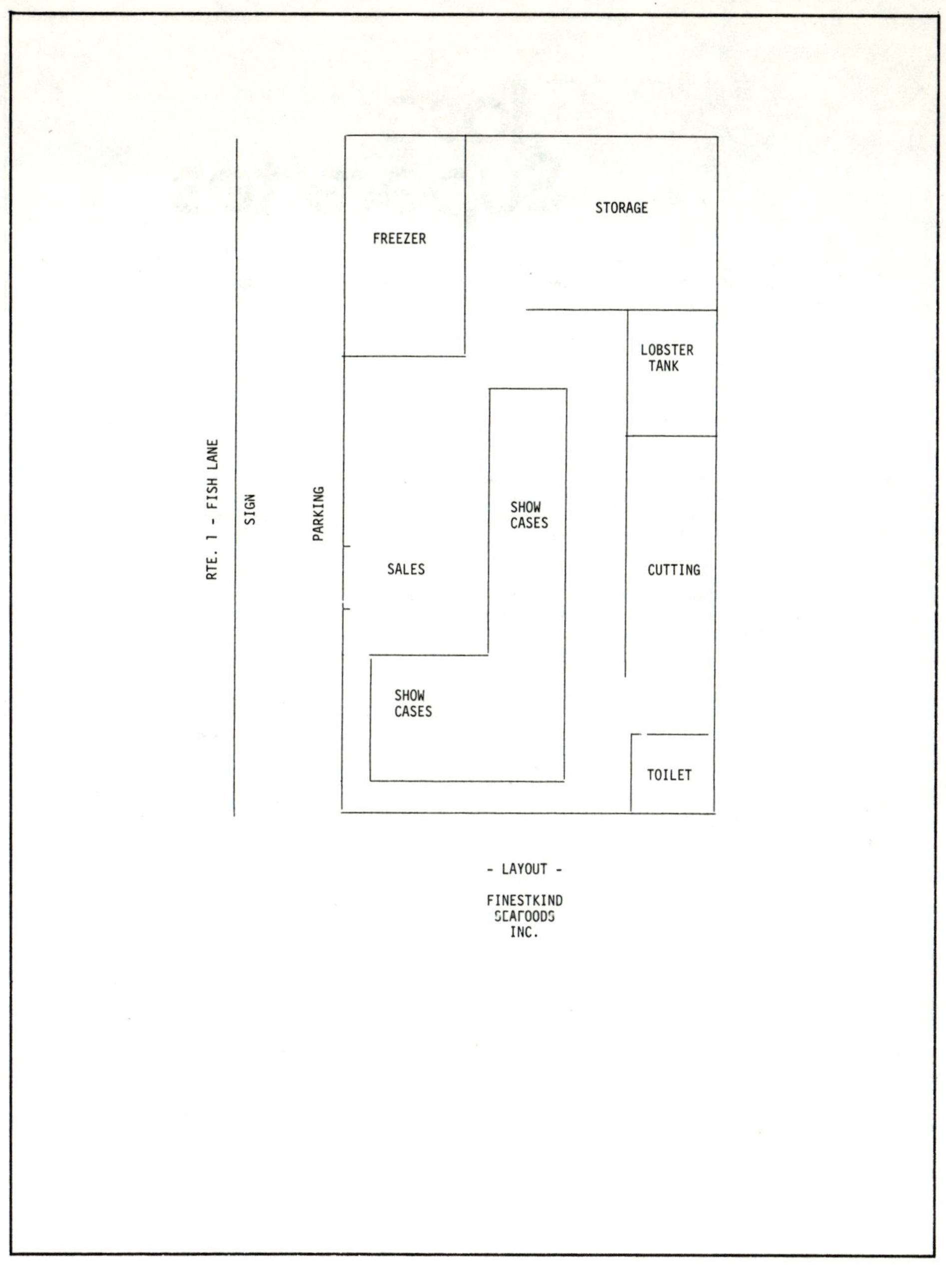
STORAGE
FREEZER
LOBSTER TANK
RTE. 1 - FISH LANE
SIGN
PARKING
SHOW CASES
SALES
CUTTING
SHOW CASES
TOILET
- LAYOUT -
FINESTKIND
SEAFOODS
INC.

GRANDiose Superettes

BANGOR PORTLAND YORK PORT LOBSTER

October 13, 19-

To Whom It May Concern:

We feel that it has been a privilege to do business with Finestkind Seafoods, Inc., throughout the relatively short time that they have been in existence. We perceive a strong demand for quality fresh fish and have been unable to secure the freshness and quality we desire on a regular basis from suppliers other than Finestkind.

Finestkind has been providing the quality/freshness level we require on a consistent basis. As long as they maintain their high standards, we will be pleased to continue our business with them.

Sincerely yours,

Michael Smart

Michael Smart
President

MS:ss

-23-

WASHINGTON LICENSE 1000 MARYLAND LICENSE 2000 VIRGINIA LICENSE 3000

JOHNSON'S PLUMBING, INC.

Telephone 202/333-2222 1327 Varnum Street, Washington, D.C.

Finestkind Seafoods, Inc.
123 Fish Lane Attn: Mr. Mike Gosling September 18,19-
Port Lobster, NH 03899

Dear Mr. Smith

For the sum of $4000.00 we propose to furnish and install the plumbing and heat work as shown on your outline sketch.

All work will be guaranteed and serviced for one year from the date of completion.

Terms, We would require a down payment of $1,150.00, another payment of $1,150 when the rough plumbing and heating is completed. The balance is due upon final completion.

If the above meets with your approval, please sign and return one copy.

Signed by

Date

Thank you,

D.L. Johnson

Derek LaMont Johnson

FUNCTIONAL RESUMES

MIKE SWAN

March 19- - June 19-: Line foreman, Fatback Fishfoods, East Machias, Maine. Responsible for hiring, training and directing operations of fifteen persons in Frozen Food Filleting Department. Rescheduled work flow with resultant 30 percent increase in output per worker. Implemented new purchasing system which reduced spoilage 8 percent. Reduced personnel turnovers by working with local union for revision of company contract policy and by shifting from production line to team task approach. Recieved Grandiose Foodstuff, Inc. award for line management and was given special assignment in September 19-, to explain these changes to other line foremen at all twenty-two Fatback Fishfoods plants in New England and the Middle Atlantic States.

MIKE GOSLING

August 19- - September 19-: Self-employed carpenter. Responsibilities included cash flow forecasting, budgeting, and various other management functions needed in the operation of a single employee business. Concurrently, night courses have been taken in small business management and sales at Pig Gut State. Currently serving on the Port Lobster Zoning Board. Prior experience included a three-year term in the US Navy. Married, two children.

APPENDIXES

A. Business Plan Front Matter
B. Functional Resumes
C. Glossary
D. Suggested References
E. Sample Worksheets
F. Notes

APPENDIX A
Business Plan Front Matter

THE COVER SHEET

The cover sheet is the first part of your business plan that your reader will see. It should—

identify the business and the document;
identify the location and telephone numbers of the business or where the principals can be reached;
identify the person(s) who wrote the business plan.

The cover sheet should not be elaborate. It should be neat, attractive, and short. If you have a logo, use it.

If the plan is to be submitted as a financing proposal, use a separate cover sheet for each bank or capital source you submit it to. See the cover sheet suggested for a financing proposal in this appendix.

Sample cover sheet for a business plan

Finestkind Seafoods, Inc.
123 Fish Lane
Port Lobster, NH 03899
Telephone 603-436-6218

Business Proposal by
Mike Gosling & Mike Swan

Sample cover sheet for a financial proposal

Financing Proposal
for
Finestkind Seafoods, Inc.

To be Submitted to
The Great Bay Bank & Trust Co.
and
The Small Business Administration

Mike Gosling
Mike Swan
123 Fish Lane
Port Lobster, N.H. 03899
603-436-5218

October 31, 19-

STATEMENT OF PURPOSE

The statement of purpose is the first page of your business plan or financial proposal. It should state the objectives of the plan or financial proposal as simply as possible. The remainder of the plan is devoted to elaborating and supporting the statement of purpose. A business plan, even for a modest deal, runs to twenty or more pages. The complete Finestkind plan is included in part 3. If the plan is for your sole use, the statement should be a brief description of how you intend to use the plan once it has been developed. For example:

> This plan is to be an operating and policy guide for Finestkind Seafoods, Inc.

The deal you are proposing—the loan or investment, its use and expected effects on the business, and how you will repay it—will be supported by the rest of your plan. If you are not seeking a loan, the plan should still support and justify the use of your own money or the money of partners, friends, or family.

Keep the statement short and businesslike. It will usually be no longer than half a page, but it may be longer if necessary. Use your own judgment.

If the plan is also to be used as a financing proposal, the statement of purpose becomes more complex. It should include responses to the following questions:

1. Who is asking for money?
2. What is the business structure (i.e., sole proprietorship, partnership, corporation, Sub-Chapter S corporation)?
3. How much money is asked for?
4. What is the money needed for?
5. How will the funds benefit the business?
6. Why does the loan or investment make sense?
7. How will the money be repaid?

Much of the cash required to start a business is usually provided by the business principals themselves. However, you may need additional funds to launch your business or provide for its growth once it gets started. These outside funds may be provided in the form of either equity or debt.

Equity represents a sale of a portion of the business. The amount you have to sell to acquire the needed funds reflects the amount of risk that the investor feels is involved. If your venture seems very risky, you may have to sell a substantial share. If it is not seen as very risky, you may not have to give up so much of the ownership.

Debt represents a loan that the lender typically expects to have repaid sometime in the future. Usually, the lender expects to receive a return for the use of his funds in the form of interest. Your plan must take into account the need to repay these funds and pay the interest.

If you use an outside equity investment, you do not have to repay the funds, but you give up a share of ownership and have to share decision-making and profits. If you use debt, you must be prepared to repay the loan and pay interest. You may find that more advice on this matter will be very helpful. Your banker or accountant can provide this advice. A discussion of different types and sources of financing is included in chapter 6.

A sample statement of purpose

> Finestkind Seafoods, Inc., is seeking a loan of $36,000 to purchase equipment and inventory, purchase property and buildings at 123 Fish Lane, Port Lobster, N.H., perform necessary renovations and improvements, maintain sufficient cash reserves, and provide adequate working capital to successfully expand an existing wholesale/retail seafood market. This sum, together with the $10,000 equity investment of the principals, will be sufficient to finance transition through the expansion phase so that this recently started business can operate as an ongoing, profitable enterprise.

Notice that this sample statement of purpose contains responses to the checklist items. The last statement is mandatory. The financial community needs to be convinced that the deal is viable and wants to see a statement to that effect in writing.

The statement of purpose cannot be completed until you have calculated your capital needs. It can be written, but the exact amount needed won't be known until the projections in section E of chapter 3, financial data, are worked through.

TABLE OF CONTENTS

The table of contents should follow your statement of purpose. Your plan in three main sections:

I. The Business
II. Financial Data
III. Supporting Documents

These sections may be broken down further if it seems necessary to do so. Listing subcategories in the table of contents helps the reader find his way through a lengthy proposal. The statement of purpose has told your reader what your deal is. He may want to turn immediately to specifics, or you may want to do the same if the business plan is for your sole use.

A sample format for the table of contents

A format of this kind makes it easy to find the section of most interest to you at any given time. (You will, of course, have to fill in the actual page numbers as you go along.) The table of contents can also serve as a guide to writing and organizing your business plan.

APPENDIX B
Functional Resumes

Functional resumes are designed to provide financing agencies with the information needed to make decisions on managerial competence and experience. Ordinary resumes (such as the SBA Personal Information Sheet) can and do provide information such as job titles, dates, and salaries, but they do not answer such questions as: Did you have hiring and firing authority? Could you redesign work flow? and others.

A functional resume is usually self-designed since most jobs are not standard. The objective of this section is to help you design a functional resume which displays your experience and competence. Treat the suggestions which follow as suggestions, not ironclad rules.

A Suggested Format
RESUME OF
Your Name

1. Business Address
   Telephone Number

2. Home Address
   Telephone Number

Education

3. Most Recent Grade or Diploma Completed First

Business experience

4. Most Recent Job First (Include military experience.)

Special abilities and interests

5. Hobbies, Clubs, Civic Activities, etc.

Personal information

6. Age, Marital Status, Number of Children

References

7. Names and Addresses of References (preferably business associates)

Items 3, 4, and 5 are those which make a functional resume different from an ordinary, fact-oriented resume. They should describe education, jobs, and interests in functional terms. For example:

Standard

March 1973-June 1975: Foreman, Fatback Fishfoods, East Machias, Maine. Beginning salary $160/week, final salary $205/week.

Notice how the standard form is composed of brief detail. Contrast this with:

Functional

March 1973-June 1975: Line foreman, Fatback Fishfoods, East Machias, Maine. Responsible for hiring, training, and directing operations of fifteen persons in Frozen Food Filleting Department. Rescheduled work flow with resultant 30 percent increase in output per worker. Implemented new purchasing system which reduced spoilage 8 percent. Reduced personnel turnovers by working with local union for revision of company contract policy and by shifting from production line to team task approach. Received Grandiose Foodstuff, Inc. award for line management and was given special assignment in September 1974 to explain these changes to other line foremen at all twenty-two Fatback Fishfoods plants in New England and the Middle Atlantic states.

Your objective in items 3, 4, and 5 is to show what you have accomplished and what abilities you have demonstrated. Item 5, Special Abilities and Interests, can be used to cover nonjob achievements, interests, and skills which may or may not be directly relevant to your employment. For instance, this is where off-the-job managerial experience would be stressed (e.g., local politics, coaching, leadership of clubs).

Here are two final points. First, a good resume (functional or otherwise) should have no sizeable (more than a month) time gaps. Longer gaps create a credibility problem. Second, a good resume will do more than inform the reader of what you have done. It will also give him an understanding of what you can do, and this understanding, based on demonstrated performance, can make the difference between a positive response to a financing proposal and a negative one.

APPENDIX C
Glossary

"Acid Test" Ratio Cash plus those other assets which can be immediately converted to cash should equal or exceed current liabilities. The formula used to determine the ratio is as follows:

$$\frac{\text{cash plus receivables (net) plus marketable securities}}{\text{current liabilities}}$$

The "acid test" ratio is one of the most important credit barometers used by lending institutions, as it indicates the ability of a business enterprise to meet its current obligations.

Aging Receivables A scheduling of accounts receivable according to the length of time they have been outstanding. This shows which accounts are not being paid in a timely manner and may reveal any difficulty in collecting long-overdue receivables. This may also be an important indicator of developing cash flow problems.

Amortization To liquidate on an installment basis; the process of gradually paying off a liability over a period of time, i.e., a mortgage is amortized by periodically paying off part of the face amount of the mortgage.

Assets The valuable resources, or properties and property rights owned by an individual or business enterprise.

Balance sheet An itemized statement which lists the total assets and the total liabilities of a given business to portray its net worth at a given moment in time.

Break-even analysis A method used to determine the point at which the business will neither make a profit nor incur a loss. That point is expressed in either the total dollars of revenue exactly offset by total expenses (fixed and variable); or in total units of production, the cost of which exactly equals the income derived by their sale.

Capital Capital funds are those funds which are needed for the base of the business. Usually they are put into the business in a fairly permanent form such as in fixed assets, plant and equipment, or they are used in other ways which are not recoverable in the short run unless you sell the entire business.

Capital equipment Equipment which you use to manufacture a product, provide a service, or use to sell, store, and deliver merchandise. Such equipment will not be sold in the normal course of business, but will be used and worn out or be consumed over time as you do business.

Cash flow The actual movement of cash within a business: cash inflow minus cash outflow. A term used to designate the reported net income of a corporation plus amounts charged off for depreciation, depletion, amortization, and extraordinary charges to reserves, which are bookkeeping deductions and not actually paid out in cash. Used to offer a better indication of the ability of a firm to meet its own obligations and to pay dividends than with the conventional net income figure.

Cash position See Liquidity

Construction loans These loans are like a line of credit crossed with a term loan: as construction of, say, a building, reaches certain stages, the bank disburses money which is repayable over a lengthy period of time, usually in a flat monthly payment, though sometimes in a balloon payment which must be refinanced.

Corporation An artificial legal entity created by government grant and endowed with certain powers; a voluntary organization of persons, either actual individuals or legal entities, legally bound together to form a business enterprise.

Credit Credit generally means trade credit unless stated otherwise, the accounts payable which your suppliers and others may be willing to extend to your business. The credit terms are usually stated on the invoice as payment due within so many days, perhaps with a discount (reduced cost) available for early payment, and with added costs for paying later than the due date on the invoice. Trade credit is one of the major sources of financing for small businesses, and, for a stable small business, may be the major form of outside financing.

Current assets Cash or other items that will normally be turned into cash within one year and assets that will be used up in the operations of a firm within one year.

Current liabilities Amounts owed that will ordinarily be paid by a firm within one year. Such items include accounts payable, wages payable, taxes payable, the current portion of a long-term debt, and interest and dividends payable.

Current ratio A ratio of a firm's current assets to its current liabilities. The current ratio includes the value of inventories which have not yet been sold, so it is not the best evaluation of the current status of the firm. The "acid test" ratio, covering the most liquid of current assets, provides a better evaluation.

Deal A proposal for financing business creation or expansion; a series of transactions and preparation of documents in order to obtain funds for business expansion or creation.

Debt Debt refers to borrowed funds, whether from your own coffers or from other individuals, banks, or other institutions. It is generally secured with a note, which in turn may be secured by a lien against property or other assets. Ordinarily, the note states repayment and interest provisions, which vary greatly in both amount and duration depending upon the purpose, source, and terms of the loan. Some debt is convertible; that is, it may be changed into direct ownership of a portion of a business under certain stated conditions.

Depreciation A reduction in the value of fixed assets. The most important causes of depreciation are wear and tear, the effect of the elements, and gradual obsolescence which makes it unprofitable to continue using some assets until they have been exhausted. The purpose of the bookkeeping charge for depreciation is to write off the original cost of an asset (less expected salvage value) by equitably distributing charges against operations over its entire useful life.

Entrepreneur An innovator of a business enterprise who recognizes opportunities to introduce a new product, a new production process, or an improved organization; and who raises the necessary money, assembles the factors of production, and organizes an operation to exploit the opportunity.

Equity Equity or net worth is the owner's investment in the business. Unlike capital, equity is what remains after the liabilities of the company are subtracted from the assets. Thus it may be greater than or less than the capital invested in the business. Equity investment carries with it a share of ownership and usually a share in profits, as well as some say in how the business is managed. If you seek financing from outside investors, you may well find that the cost is parting with some equity; this sometimes is viewed as a threat to ownership even though effective control usually remains in the hands of the owner/manager.

Illiquid See Liquidity

Line of credit Either secured or unsecured, an agreement which ordinarily is renewed on an annual basis where a bank holds funds available for the use of a business. Usually an unsecured line will have to be completely paid out once a year. The advantage of a line of credit is that the money is there, ready to be used when needed, yet not costing more than a slight fee until it is actually drawn upon. Your credit card is a line of credit: it allows you to borrow up to so many dollars and make repayment in a pre-agreed fashion. No separate credit application is made at each use of the line. A line of credit is usually paid from normal operations; inventory is often seasonally financed under a line of credit, for example.

Liquidity A term used to describe the solvency of a business, and which has special reference to the degree of readiness in which assets can be converted into cash without a loss. Also called *cash position.* If a firm's current assets cannot be converted into cash to meet current liabilities, the firm is said to be *illiquid.*

Loan agreement A document which states repayment terms, interest rates, and usually, what a business can or cannot do as long as it owes money to (usually) a bank. A loan agreement may place restrictions on owner's salary, on dividends, on amount of other debt, on working capital limits, on sales, on number of added personnel, or whatever the lender views as a means of protecting his investment. It is helpful to note that while equity ordinarily controls a company, a loan agreement ensures that a large degree of control passes into the hands of the lender. This kind of agreement is frequently a condition of making a loan.

Loans Debt money for small business is usually in the form of bank loans, loans which in a real sense are personal loans because a new small business is hard to evaluate in terms of credit-worthiness and degree of risk, the two decisive variables in any judgment of making or not making a loan. A *secured* loan is a loan which is backed up by a claim against some asset or assets of a business; an *unsecured* loan is backed up by the faith the bank has in the borrower's ability to pay the money back. All loans fall into one of these categories. *Note:* the amount of collateral (assets securing the loan) asked for should always be considered—too much collateralization will tie your hands in the future. The purpose of collateral, incidentally, is to tie you to the deal, to make it hard for you to walk away if things get rough. Banks have no desire to become secondhand business-collateral dealers, and even less desire to pull the personal assets of your cosigners or comakers. (Many bankers don't know this. They think, erroneously, that by securing the note with collateral they are making the loan "safer." They aren't.)

Long-term liabilities Liabilities (expenses) which will not mature within the next year.

Market The number of people and their total spending (actual or potential) for your product line within the geographic limits of your distribution ability. The market share is the percentage of your sales compared to the sales of your competitors in total for a particular product line.

Note The basic business loan, a note, represents a loan which will be repaid or substantially reduced thirty, sixty or ninety days later at a stated interest rate. These are short-term, and, unless they are made under a line of credit, a separate loan application is needed for each loan and each renewal.

Net worth The owners' equity in a given business represented by the excess of the total assets over the total amounts owing to outside creditors (total liabilities) at a given moment in time. Also, the net worth of an individual as determined by deducting the amount of all his personal liabilities from the total value of his personal assets.

Partnership A legal relationship created by the voluntary association of two or more persons to carry on as co-owners of a business for profit; a type of business organization in which two or more persons agree on the amount of their contributions (capital and effort) and on the distribution of profits, if any.

Pro forma A projection or estimate of what may result in the future from actions in the present. A pro forma financial statement is one that shows how the actual operations of the business will turn out if certain assumptions are realized.

Profit The excess of the selling price over all costs and expenses incurred in making the sale. Also, the reward to the entrepreneur for the risks assumed by him in the establishment, operation, and management of a given enterprise or undertaking.

Revolving line of credit Similar to a line of credit, except it needn't be paid out annually. This kind of loan is of particular interest to a rapidly growing company with weak capitalization and may be converted to a term loan under certain conditions. But its basic purpose is the same as a line of credit.

Sole proprietorship or proprietorship A type of business organization in which one individual owns the business. Legally, the owner is the business and personal assets are typically exposed to liabilities of the business.

Sub-chapter S corporation or tax option corporation A corporation which has selected under Sub-Chapter S of the IRS Tax Code (by unanimous consent of its shareholders) not to pay any corporate tax on its income and, instead, to have the shareholders pay taxes on it, even though it is not distributed. Shareholders of a tax-option corporation are also entitled to deduct, on the individual returns, their shares of any net operating loss sustained by the corporation, subject to limitations in the tax code. In many respects, Sub-Chapter S permits a corporation to behave for tax purposes as a proprietorship or partnership.

Subordinated debt Subordinated debt is sometimes referred to as *quasi-capital* because it serves the same purposes as capital as far as a bank is concerned. Subordinating debt means placing that particular debt behind bank debt; that is, should your business go bust and have to be sold for asset value, your bank gets paid before the holder of the subordinated debt. Often, the owners of a business will put loans made by them to the company in such a position; it means that until the bank debt is paid off or reduced to a previously agreed amount, the owners cannot repay themselves.

Take-over The acquisition of one company by another company.

Target market The specific individuals, distinguished by socio-economic, demographic, and/or interest characteristics, who are the most likely potential customers for the goods and/or services of a business.

Term loans Either secured or unsecured, usually for periods of more than a year to as many as twenty years. Term loans are paid off like a mortgage: so many dollars per month for so many years. The most common uses of term loans are for equipment and other fixed asset purposes, for working capital, and for real estate. Ordinarily, businesses do not borrow for a year or less on a term basis; the cost to the bank would be excessive.

Working capital By definition, this is the difference between current assets and current liabilities. Contrasted with capital, a permanent use of funds, working capital is for relatively short-term use. Working capital cycles through your business in a variety of forms: inventories, accounts and notes receivable, cash and securities, prepaid expenses are but a few. Working capital shifts forms but remains an investment in and use of cash. Working capital may fluctuate in terms of seasonal needs. If you have an inventory build-up prior to Christmas sales or to your fall merchandising season, then the cash portion of your working capital will be reduced; as you sell off the inventory and retire your payables, your cash will increase. Due to this seasonal quality of working capital in some industries, it is wrong to rely too heavily on trade averages unless you know what point in the working capital cycle they come from.

APPENDIX D
Suggested References

The following list is necessarily arbitrary and short. For a more complete bibliography, ask your banker, your nearest SBA office, public and college librarians, trade journals, and experienced businesspersons.

Annual Statement Studies, published by Robert Morris Associates, Credit Division, Philadelphia National Bank Building, Philadelphia, Pennsylvania 19107.

Barometer of Small Business, published semiannually by the Accounting Corporation of America, 1929 First Avenue, San Diego, California 92101.

Business Resource Directory, Urban Affairs Section, Federal Reserve Bank of Boston, 2nd edition, 1975. This 260-page handbook lists sources of free and low-cost technical assistance for New England business people. Groups are arranged by state and city and are cross-indexed according to the type of services they provide. The publication is free and may be obtained by writing to Business Resource Directory, Urban Affairs, Federal Reserve Bank of Boston, 600 Atlantic Avenue, Boston, Massachusetts 02106. Other areas may have similar publications.

How to Organize and Operate a Small Business, Clifford Baumback, Kenneth Lawyer, and Pearce Kelley, 5th edition, Prentice-Hall, Inc., Englewood Cliffs, New Jersey, 1973. This book is an outstanding source of information and is used widely as a text. In addition to providing an in-depth overview of small business operation and policy, it includes an excellent topical bibliography. You will probably find this in your library.

Small Business Reporter, Department 3120, Bank of America, P.O. Box 37000, San Francisco, California 94137. $1.00 per copy. The "Business Operations" series is helpful for general information on running a business. Titles include: *Opening Your Own Business, Small Business Success, How to Buy or Sell A Business, Financing Small Business, Personnel for the Small Business, Steps to Starting A Business.* Other series are "Business Profiles," which cover specific small businesses and "Professional Management" for doctors, dentists, and veterinarians.

The Small Business Association (SBA) provides a series of pamphlets, leaflets, and booklets which are either free or available for a very slight charge. Of particular interest are the: *Starting and Managing Series, Small Business Management Series,* and *Ratio Analysis for Small Businesses.* These booklets contain a wealth of advice for prices ranging from $.45 to $1.80.

Aids Annuals contain more information at prices up to $1.25 per volume. These include information for small businesses, small manufacturers, and small marketers. *Aids* for the current year are available at no cost. *Suggested Management Guides* ($1.25), *Managing for Profits* ($.65), and *Buying and Selling a Small Business* are non-series publications that are excellent general information sources. You can get a list of all SBA publications from your nearest SBA office, or write to Small Business Administration, Superintendent of Documents, Government Printing Office, Washington, D.C. 20402.

Urban Business Profile Series, published by the U.S. Department of Commerce, Washington, D.C. 20230, is another useful reference for new and small businesses.

APPENDIX E
Sample Worksheets

The following sample worksheets will be useful for you and those involved in your business to fill out. They provide important information in a concise manner. That information in turn may be incorporated into your business plan or financial proposal. These worksheets may be reproduced, or you can work up similar ones that focus on areas especially important to your business plan.

PERSONAL DATA SHEET

Name ________________ Birthdate ________________
Address ________________ Tel. No. ________________ Years there ________________
Business Address ________________ Phone ________________
Marital Status ________________ Name of Spouse ________________ Dependents ________________

Education ________ Name ________________ Grade completed-program-degree? ________________
Address ________________
Military Service ________________ Highest Rank Obtained ____ Years ________________
Relevant Training or Work Experience ________________
____

Work Experience
Business and Address ________________
Job Titles and Duties ________________
Supervisor ________________
Dates ________________
Reasons for Leaving ________________
Trade, Professional, or Civic Membership and Activities ________________
____
____

Hobbies, Interests, Other Relevant Information ________________
____
____

Use second sheet if necessary.

CREDIT INQUIRY

Name____
Address ____________________ Years here___ Phone ______________
Former address ___________________________Years here ___________
Birth date__________ Marital status__________No. of dependents________
Employer ____________________Years here___ Phone ______________
Address _______________________________ Kind of bus.____________
Position _______________________________Net income $/__________
Former employer & address _______________________ Years here _______
Name of spouse ____
Spouse's employer & address________________________ Net income $/_____
Other income source ______________ $ per month __________________
Bank_____________ Acct. # ______________Balance______________
Checking acct.____
Savings acct. ____
Auto owned (yr. and make) __________ Purchased from _______$ _________
Financed by______________________Balance owing $ _______ Monthly______
Rent or mortgage payment $ __________paid to______________________
Real estate owned in name of __________ Purchase price $ ________Mtge. Bal. ____

Credit references and all debts owing (other than above)
(Bank, loan or finance co's., credit unions, budget)

Name	Address	Orig. Amt.	Bal.	Mo. Payment

Life insurance amt. $ ______________Co. ___________________________
If comaker for others, state where and for whom _____________________
Nearest relative or friend not living with you _______________________
Relationship ____
Address ____

APPENDIX F
Notes

As you work with this book, and as you develop your own business plan and finance proposal, you will want a record of the data you gather. The following pages are provided for your use. Collect your information and ideas here; reference key items back to relevant sections in this book if you wish. These pages will become your information resource for your business and its future.

Notes

Notes

Notes

Notes

Notes